THE CLARENDON BIOGRAPHIES

General Editors: C. L. MOWAT and M. R. PRICE

KEIR HARDIE

by

Kenneth O. Morgan

Fellow of The Queen's College, Oxford

OXFORD UNIVERSITY PRESS

1967

Oxford University Press, Ely House, London, W.1

GLASGOW NEW YORK TORONTO MELBOURNE WELLINGTON
CAPE TOWN SALISBURY IBADAN NAIROBI LUSAKA ADDIS ABABA
BOMBAY CALCUTTA MADRAS KARACHI LAHORE DACCA
KUALA LUMPUR HONG KONG TOKYO

Printed in Great Britain by Richard Clay (The Chaucer Press), Ltd.,
Bungay, Suffolk

CONTENTS

LIST OF ILLUSTRATIONS

ACKNOWLEDGEMENT

THE author would like to acknowledge the generous assistance he received while writing this book from the Research Fund of the University College of Swansea.

1

THE YOUNG REBEL (1856–87)

THE life of Keir Hardie has become part of the saga of the British labour movement. For many it has passed from history into legend. Long before his death in 1915, Hardie had attained a kind of heroic stature. His portrait had replaced those of the Queen or Mr. Gladstone upon the walls of many a humble miner's cottage. After his death, accounts of his career became increasingly mythical. Ramsay MacDonald, later to become the first Labour Prime Minister in 1924, could compare him to a new Moses, leading the children of labour out of bondage towards a better society. No other working-class leader in British history has inspired quite the same devotion. Fifty years after his death, his name can reduce the Labour Party Conference or the Trades Union Congress to rapturous enthusiasm. For them, it seems, he has become and will always remain one of the saints who from their labours rest.

Of course, the real Keir Hardie was much more complicated. Like Gandhi and other apparently saintly figures, Hardie was also a very shrewd politician, with a subtle appreciation of the arts of the possible. He made bitter enemies as well as devoted admirers. For much of his life, as *The Times* noted in its obituary, he had been one of the most hated men of his day, a rebel, a fanatic, even perhaps a traitor. From a distance, Hardie might seem a pillar of moral righteousness. At close quarters, he could often appear obstinate, vain, or unreliable. Even so, the legend of Hardie's life and struggles retains its vital core of truth. It remains a moving document of how a poor, uneducated Scottish boy could rise to the heights of political leadership. Further, Hardie's career symbolizes a wider social revolution in Britain which has, in the past fifty years, made our society more just and more satisfying for the ordinary working people of the land.

Although Hardie finished his days in 1915 as a broken and dis-illusioned man, the principles for which he fought lived on, and have been decisive in the making of the Britain of today.

James Keir Hardie was born amid desperate poverty in Leg-brannock, a village in the Lanarkshire coalfield in western Scot-land, on 15 August 1856. The industrial power and prosperity of Victorian Britain seemed to be at their height: only five years earlier, the Great Exhibition at the Crystal Palace had proclaimed them to the world. But little enough of this was to be seen in Legbrannock. Hardie's home was a tiny, one-roomed cottage, with thatched roof, whitewashed walls, and a floor of baked mud. Hardie's father, whom he never knew, was an unemployed miner; his mother, Mary Keir, was a farm-servant and the daughter of a widow. Like Ramsay MacDonald and Ernest Bevin among labour leaders, Hardie was an illegitimate child, a social outcast from the very beginning. Shortly after his birth, his mother married David Hardie, a ship's carpenter. It was thus as Keir Hardie that young James was henceforth known through-out his childhood and subsequent career.

It was a time of trade depression in the western Scottish coal-field. Soon the Hardie family moved to Govan, near Glasgow, to seek work in the great shipyards of the Clyde. Like other working-class boys, Keir Hardie was sent out to work at the earliest op-portunity. At the tender age of eight, he began work as a mes-senger boy for a shipping firm; by the time he was ten, he had already been through a long series of harsh, unrewarding occupa-tions. One incident that made a deep impression upon him came in 1866, when he was ten. His stepfather was out of work, his young brother critically ill, and the family virtually dependent on Hardie's wages of 3s. 6d. for a twelve-and-a-half-hour day. He worked at this time for a baker, a prominent local man, a pillar of the Church and the Sunday School. One day, young James arrived for work fifteen minutes late; in fact, he had been tending his sick younger brother. His employer dismissed him at once, without listening to any explanation. This experience did not attract young James to employers as a class, especially when they confined their professed Christian principles to Sundays alone.

The family moved back to Lanarkshire. They took up a cottage in 'The Quarter', an old community of near-slum cottages near Hamilton. By now they numbered four boys and two girls, with the eleven-year-old James as the major breadwinner. Inevitably, he went down the pit. His first job was to be that of a 'trapper', letting in the air to ventilate the mine shaft; 'Trapper' was to be his pen-name in the Press in later years. At the age of twelve, he was put in charge of a pit-pony. He graduated to become an ordinary collier, working hard twelve hours a day with a pick on the coal-face. Here, he experienced all the terrors of life underground, the rock falls and explosions that killed without warning. He continued as a miner until the age of twenty-three. These years made him deeply aware of the poverty which formed the lot of so many working-class families. Conditions for miners were hard. There was no basic wage, and pay could fall to as little as 2s. 6d. a day. Men could work as much as a twelve-hour day underground, while a sudden slump in trade could mean instant unemployment, with no social insurance for protection. In a real sense, Hardie was to remain a miner all his life, deeply wedded to the values and fellowship of a closely-knit mining community. It was fitting that in the last fifteen years of his life he should represent a South Wales mining seat in Parliament. From this time also, derived the physical ill-health that was to plague Hardie's middle age and to bring him to a premature death.

But he was far from being just an ordinary Scottish miner. He had, in particular, a deeply abiding passion for education. He attended Fraser's night school in Holytown after his day's work, but his main education came from his own efforts alone. He taught himself to read, and, with much more difficulty, to write. While working underground, he taught himself Pitman's short-hand, picking out the characters on a blackened slate with a pin used by miners to adjust the wicks of their lamps. Soon he was immersing himself in Scottish history and poetry, romantic stories of Bruce and Wallace from the Middle Ages, border ballads from a later period. The most intense impression upon him was undoubtedly made by the poetry of Robert Burns. Hardie later claimed that his own socialism derived far more from the simple democratic humanity of Burns than from all the complex theories of philosophers and economists. Burns's creed of human comradeship summed up Hardie's own instincts:

> Man to man the world over
> Shall brothers be for all that.

Now and later, Hardie remained very much the patriotic Scotsman. It was the Scottish labour movement that was to provide the framework for his social and political outlook. The Scots, like the Welsh later on, he thought were natural socialists, with their traditions of social co-operation. Many leaders of the Independent Labour Party in its earliest years were Scotsmen: Ramsay MacDonald, Bruce Glasier, Robert Smillie, and later James Maxton. The Party had stronger roots in Scotland than in any other part of the United Kingdom.

In addition to this Scottish heritage, Hardie's other main inspiration came from religion. This was also to affect his ideals profoundly. Although his parents were atheists, the young Hardie found deep solace in reading the Bible. He was stirred by the simple ethics of the Sermon on the Mount, with its message of hope for the poor and the meek, and the contrast with the injustices of the real world he saw around him in Lanark and beyond. He became a member of the Band of Hope, and remained all his life an ardent enemy of drink as a menace to the progress of the working man. As he put it, 'Liquor and Labour don't mix.' He also joined the 'Morrisonians', a small evangelical sect which believed that the salvation or damnation of men lay not in God's will but in their own efforts. Ministers of religion and their congregations were often to disappoint Hardie, but the simple message of the carpenter's son of Nazareth provided the mainspring of his socialist creed. It added a distinct strain of puritanism to the many elements that were to make up the Labour Party. Socialism was less a code of ideas than a religious gospel, with Hardie himself as its prophet among men.

As soon as he grew up to manhood, Hardie became actively involved in Scottish trade unionism. There was in the 1870s virtually no unionism at all among the Scottish miners, apart from a small body in the Kinross and Fife coalfield. It was hard to weld the scattered village pits into a wider unity. Hardie quickly became an active propagandist among the Lanarkshire miners; he campaigned tirelessly on behalf of Alexander McDonald, the veteran miners' leader. In 1879, at the age of twenty-three, Hardie was made secretary of the Hamilton miners, but the very next day was dismissed by his own employer. Instead, he managed to start up a small village shop, which was kept going by the purchases of well-wishers. In August of the same year, he was appointed agent for the Lanarkshire miners. A year later, in August 1880, came a decisive turning-point in his life. He led the Lanarkshire miners in their first-ever strike against the owners. It was a protest against starvation wages, which had fallen to less than 2s. a day. During the weeks that the strike lasted, many miners experienced, almost for the first time, the daily delights of sunshine and fresh air. They kept themselves going on potatoes or 'tatties', and the 'tattie strike' passed into popular legend. After a month, the miners were forced to return to work, but a new spirit had arisen in the western Scottish coalfield. There could, however, be no place for an agitator like Hardie in the Lanarkshire mines henceforth, since the coal-owners there refused to employ him. Almost immediately he was invited to serve as secretary of the self-styled Miners' Union in neighbouring Ayrshire. In this capacity, he first made his name as a young rebel on the national stage.

For a time, however, he faced very severe financial difficulties. He had lost his job as a working miner, since no owner would risk taking him on. Further, in 1882 the Ayrshire miners found themselves unable to pay his salary. To make ends meet, he took on a temporary post as a reporter in a local newspaper, the *Cumnock News*, published in a small mining community in southern Ayrshire. It was Hardie's first real taste of journalism. He was not a natural writer, yet his directness and sincerity were to make him an effective one. For the next thirty years he was to use the

printed word almost as effectively as the public platform in
making converts to socialism. But he still lived from hand to
mouth on a meagre income. He was now a married man, his wife
being Lillie Wilson, whom he had met during work in the temperance movement. A patient and self-effacing woman, Mrs.
Hardie was to share many of the struggles and the hardships of
her husband's career. They were to have three surviving children,
two sons and a daughter. They settled down in Cumnock (or Old
Cumnock as it was then called), eventually moving into a house
named 'Lochnorris', a solid, stone, six-roomed building that still
stands on a bend in the Auchinleck road leading northwards out
of Cumnock towards Kilmarnock. Eighty years later, 'Lochnorris'
was still owned by the Hardie family; the study there contained
a fascinating collection of mementoes of Hardie's travels in different parts of the world. Throughout his later life, Hardie returned home to Cumnock whenever he could; here alone, perhaps, his spirit found peaceful release from the storms that beset
his public career.

However, in the 1880s most of his energies here were spent in
industrial agitation, in trying to spur the miners on somehow
into united action. At last, in 1886, he found a regular job. A new
Miners' Union was formed for Ayrshire, this time on a permanent
basis, and Hardie became its first secretary—at the princely salary
of £75 a year. The years of direst poverty were over. Shortly afterwards, he took on the secretaryship of the new Scottish Miners'
Federation, which added just £5 to his annual income. Finan-
cially, his position was uncertain for some years more, but at least
he now had a permanent industrial base.

From this time onwards, the name of Keir Hardie became more
and more notorious in Scotland as a stormy petrel. He had hitherto been absorbed in industrial agitation alone, since it was here
he believed that the main struggle of labour lay. In politics, he
had always considered himself a Liberal, though one of advanced
views. But now his opinions veered sharply to the left. He had
been much impressed by a Scottish lecture tour of the American
radical, Henry George, in 1884. George urged that only a single
tax on land would undermine the monopoly of land ownership,

which he held was the greatest single cause of poverty. His argu-
ments had a ready appeal in Scotland where so much of the coalfield was in the hands of absentee 'lairds'. At this time also,
Hardie met several members of socialist organizations. Among
them was James Patrick of the Social Democratic Federation, a
body formed by H. M. Hyndman in 1881 which supported Marx's
creed of revolutionary socialism. These were years of growing
industrial turbulence throughout many parts of Britain. Unemployment was rising ominously; the crisis was heightened when
demonstrators clashed fiercely with the police in meetings in
Trafalgar Square in 1886 and 1887. Hardie was deeply stirred by
these events; not for nothing was he later to be known in parliament as 'member for the unemployed'. He was also much impressed by socialist leaders such as the Londoner, John Burns,
later to be his bitter foe but in the 1880s a great champion of
labour.

Hardie's sharpening political awareness found a platform in
The Miner, a monthly newspaper he founded in 1887; in 1889 it
changed its name to the better-known *Labour Leader*. Here,
Hardie launched a bitter attack on the industrial system. In the
foreword to the first issue of his new journal, he wrote: 'The
whole system on which wages are paid is rotten to the core. . . .
The labourer and the capitalist are partners in the working of a
concern. Why should all profit go to the one, while the other
starves?' He bitterly denounced the miners' spokesmen in Parliament, all of whom were respectable Liberals. Some of them even
opposed the eight-hour day because they claimed it would lead
to reduced wages for their men. Hardie urged that the moral was
that the miners should send more representatives to Westminster,
and demand a less servile approach from them. It was absurd, now
that tens of thousands of miners had obtained the vote by the
1884 Reform Act, that there should be a mere half-a-dozen
miners' members in the House of Commons. Without an effective
voice at Westminster, miners as a class would remain powerless
and leaderless. To further this end, Hardie himself was nomin-
ated by the Ayrshire miners as parliamentary candidate for North
Ayrshire in 1887, his first venture into politics.

At this time, he established many of the contacts and friendships which were to help him build up the labour movement in Scotland and beyond. He formed firm friendships, for instance, with other young Scots rebels such as Bruce Glasier and Bob Smillie. With Smillie, he paid his first visit to London in 1887 as part of a trade union delegation. The trip was marred only when Hardie led his friends hopelessly astray on the wrong bus, during a sight-seeing tour. Another Scottish friend, David Lowe, gives us, in his *Memoirs of Scottish Labour,* a portrait of Hardie's appearance at this time. He was a man only of medium height, but with exceptionally broad chest and back. Most conspicuous were the sensitive hazel eyes, the massive forehead, framed by flowing hair, and the bushy red beard which was soon to make him famous. His appearance was dramatic, unconventional; he seemed part Scottish miner, part romantic poet. Already he looked much older than his thirty-one years. Years of toil at the coal-face, and the further strain of trade union agitation had taken their toll. As a public speaker he had already made his name on the open-air platform. Yet he was far from being a natural orator, hesitant in his delivery and desperately nervous. 'Speechmaking was not play to him,' observed Lowe, 'but rather a torture to body and soul.' But his passionate sincerity enabled him to drive his message home with conviction. All through his life, his oratorical style was always that of the soapbox and the outdoor meeting. In the more mannered atmosphere of the House of Commons, he was to show himself less at ease. He thrived on direct personal contact with a mass audience; he would address them, in his democratic way, as 'Men and Women', instead of the more conventional 'Ladies and Gentlemen'. Of Hardie it was indeed true that the style was the man.

Hardie first made his mark nationally at the remarkable Trades Union Congress at Swansea in 1887. For years, the trade unions had pursued a cautious policy, economically and politically. Of none was this more evident than of the miners' leaders, most of them products of the sternest brand of chapel-going Liberalism. Chief among the T.U.C. leaders was their much respected parliamentary secretary, Henry Broadhurst, M.P. To the amazement of the delegates, Hardie launched a fierce attack upon Broadhurst for knuckling under to the Liberal Party in a servile manner, and especially for opposing an eight-hour day for miners. This outburst from an unknown delegate caused a sensation. Hardie was attending the Conference for the first time; the union he represented, the Ayrshire Miners, was very small and unimportant. Broadhurst, stung by the attack, used all his authority to deflate Hardie with ridicule. 'He (Broadhurst) was amazed at a man coming here for the first time, and showing such bad taste (hear, hear).' It was a most 'un-English' outburst from 'the high priest and prophet of Ayrshire'. Broadhurst easily carried the day at Swansea.

But Hardie's stand there foretold a wider mood of radical protest. In the next seven years, as the trade depression widened, a new wave of rebellion was to grow up within the conservative membership of the T.U.C., with the little-known Hardie as one of its spearheads. More, Hardie, and other young rebels like him, were increasingly to press for the trade unions to turn to political action, as the main hope for the working class. The years heralded by the clash between Hardie and Broadhurst were to form one of the decisive turning-points in modern British history. Here indeed were the seeds of what a later historian called the 'strange death of Liberal England'. A social and political revolution was in the making, and Keir Hardie, the illegitimate, ill-educated son of a poor Lanarkshire miner, would be the man to lead it.

2

THE SOCIALIST PIONEER (1888-93)

THE decisive shift in Hardie's interests from the industrial to the political field came in April 1888, with a famous by-election at Mid-Lanark. In Scotland, as for Britain as a whole, the 1880s were a decade of exceptional turmoil and tension. The whole land seemed to be seething with a strange, new unrest. In the distant isles of the north-west, poor crofters were revolting against their lairds. Middle-class radicals in the central lowlands were preaching the cause of Scottish home rule, following upon the successful attainment of a Secretary of State for Scotland in 1885. Others were pressing for disestablishment of the Presbyterian Church, while the question of Irish home rule added a new source of fierce division. In the coalfield, as we have seen, a series of strikes and lock-outs had broken out. The whole fabric of Scottish society, as it had endured since the 1830s, dominated by a genteel brand of moderate Liberalism, seemed thrown into confusion. It was, however, Keir Hardie's intervention at Mid-Lanark that helped to provoke a new explosion.

Hitherto, Hardie had always thought of himself as a staunch supporter of Gladstone, 'the Grand Old Man'. But the continuing failure of the Liberals to support a miners' eight-hour day and other social reforms gradually led him to the reluctant conclusion that over the fundamental issues of the day Liberals and Conservatives were virtually identical in their views. This was put to the test at Mid-Lanark in the spring of 1888. When a by-election was announced there, Hardie offered his name to the Liberal Association, but was curtly rejected in favour of Wynford Philipps, a wealthy Welsh barrister imported from London. Hardie then announced his intention of fighting the seat as an independent working-class candidate, an action almost without precedent in the history of Scottish politics. The central Liberal party organization tried desperately to persuade him to withdraw his candidature: it threatened a split in the Liberal vote which might let the Conservative in. However, he refused all Liberal inducements, even the offer of a safe seat elsewhere and a salary of £300 a year. Long afterwards, writing in the *Labour Leader*, Hardie cheerfully listed this among 'Bribes I have been offered'. He well knew how the parrot cry of 'Tory gold' had told against socialist candidates in the recent past. Liberal gold was no better. He therefore took great pains to protect his independence, though in fact much of his campaign fund was raised by H. H. Champion, a socialist of Tory inclinations.

Hardie made it abundantly clear that he was fighting as an

independent Labour candidate. Yet, confusingly, he still claimed
to be a supporter of Gladstone and the Liberals. The word
'socialist' never appeared on his manifesto. His support at Mid-
Lanark came from a bewildering variety of groups, land reformers
from the Highlands, trade unionists from the Glasgow slums,
Scottish home rulers in Edinburgh (and in London, where they
were led by a young man named Ramsay MacDonald). Hardie's
campaign workers included some colourful individuals. There
was the radical landowner, R. B. Cunninghame-Graham, who
had created a spectacular reputation on the South American pam-
pas, as 'Don Roberto'. Again there was Michael Davitt, a fervent
Irish nationalist and leader of the militant Land League, with
whom Hardie's relations went through many fluctuations.
Hardie's agent was Champion, the son of an Indian army officer,
who had himself resigned his commission a few years earlier and
was soon to emigrate to Australia. It was difficult, perhaps im-
possible, to work out a positive creed that bound together these
different elements. Essentially, it was dissatisfaction with Liberalism that gave them a platform, rather than a positive belief in
Socialism, a vague feeling that there ought to be more working
men in Parliament, rather than the urge to found a separate
political party. The vision of a 'Labour Party' was still very
remote.

Hardie's programme at Mid-Lanark included some highly
radical proposals. In addition to home rule for Ireland (and for
Scotland), and social and economic measures such as the miners'
eight-hour day and nationalization of the mines, he also bitterly
denounced the money spent (or wasted) on the monarchy. This
last was a particularly unpopular view, since the Queen's spectacular golden jubilee the previous year was still fresh in the
memory. Hardie found his campaign among the scattered Lanarkshire villages to be hard going indeed. In particular, the Irish
voters there, who were quite numerous, voted heavily for the
Liberal (and therefore for Gladstone), despite all Davitt's urgings
that the Irish and the working class shared a common cause.
Hardie was a victim of that religious antagonism between Protestant and 'Papist' still familiar to supporters of Glasgow football

teams. On paper the result was most disappointing. Philipps, the Liberal, won comfortably from the Conservative. Hardie polled a mere 617 votes (the 'gallant six hundred' he called them), and finished at the bottom of the poll.

But the forces released at Mid-Lanark were rapidly gaining in strength. The next month, in May 1888, a new 'Scottish Labour Party' was formed in Glasgow by Cunninghame-Graham and other radicals. In August, Hardie became its secretary. Its pro-gramme was vague in some respects. While it demanded national-ization of the coal-mines, of land, and of the railways, it carefully refrained from calling itself a socialist party. It also refused to challenge the Liberals directly, after the recent experience at Mid-Lanark. Its members, rather, hoped for local pacts to sponsor working-class candidates. For many years, it remained a small and divided organization with perhaps a couple of hundred mem-bers; it finally merged into the I.L.P. in 1894. Yet, during its six short years of life, it was to form a basis for the Independent Labour Party. It symbolized the growing tension between classes which was making the gulf between Labour and Liberals ever wider.

Hardie was now more and more prominent in pushing forward radical demands at the annual T.U.C. As delegate of the Ayrshire Miners, he led the fight for an eight-hour day; indeed, it was this issue as much as any other that clarified his retreat from his former Liberalism. His voice was a less lonely one now. His attacks on Broadhurst and the old guard of trade union leaders found wider and wider support. These were years of immense upheaval for British trade unionists. Previously, only a small proportion of working men had been trade union members—perhaps no more than a tenth in all. They were usually men in skilled trades, crafts-men with a privileged position to uphold, who regarded them-selves as 'the aristocracy of labour'. But from the late 1880s came a very important movement usually called 'the new unionism'. It was much stimulated by the great London Dock Strike of 1889, when sympathy for the 'dockers' tanner' (i.e. a basic wage of 6d. an hour) swept the country. As a result, many thousands of un-skilled workers, dockers, gasworkers, building workers, and

Keir Hardie in 1892 as 'Queer Hardie'.

VOTE FOR

Home Rule.

Democratic
Government.

Justice to Labour

No Monopoly.

No Landlordism

Temperance
Reform.

Healthy Home

Fair Rents.

Eight-Hour Da

Work for th
Unemployed

KEIR HARDIE

Printed and Published by F W. Scross & Co. [L S.C.], 151, Barking Road, Canning Town, London, E.

Hardie's election poster at West Ham in 1895.

HARDIE'S HERALD

'The class which makes a
nation's Laws
Will also own its Wealth."

"Our cause is the cause of
the ages,
Our hope is the hope of the
World."

AND EAST BRADFORD CAMPAIGNER.

No. 3.   Wednesday, November 4th, 1896.   PRICE ONE HALFPENNY.

LANDLORD & CAPITALIST FLOURISH

AT THE EXPENSE OF LABOUR.

Meade Collection

Hardie's Herald: East Bradford by-election, 1896.

NOT A WISE SAW

Mr. Keir Hardie wishes to make Labour representation entirely independent of the Liberal Party.

Top: Severance from the Liberal Party, 1903.
Above: Police defending power-house, Tonypandy riot, 1910.

general labourers were caught up in a new wave of unionism. They were usually more militant than the older unions, since the cyclical slumps of depression and unemployment of the 1880s bore most harshly upon them. Most of their leaders were openly committed socialists, men like Ben Tillett of the dockers, and Tom Mann of the engineers. As the 'new unionists' poured into the trade union movement, the age-old attitudes of the T.U.C. were transformed.

At the Dundee T.U.C. in 1889, Hardie found surprising support in his demand for more labour representation in Parliament. A clash with another Scotsman, Chisholm Robertson, who accused Hardie of using non-union labour in printing election propaganda, emphasized that he was now the most hated and feared man in the Congress. The next year, the Congress was held in Liverpool, a stronghold of the 'new unionism' with its large Irish population. For the first time, and by the narrow margin of only eight votes, the T.U.C. upheld the demand for a miners' eight-hour day. In the 1891 Congress at Newcastle this decision was confirmed, and Hardie's amendment to make the eight-hour day compulsory, save where the workers voted otherwise, was carried overwhelmingly by 285 votes to 183. Events had moved fast since Hardie had been howled down at Swansea four years earlier. From now on, the miners' eight-hour day was official T.U.C. policy until it finally became law in 1909. In practice, the agitation for it helped to underline dissatisfaction with 'Lib.–Lab.' policies and to spur on the cause of socialism.

Hardie had so far been known primarily as a spokesman for Scottish labour. He was still comparatively unknown in England. But already there were signs of a wider sympathy in which Hardie's name would become renowned throughout the world as one of the leading spokesmen for international socialism. In 1889 he went abroad for the first time, to attend the first congress of the Second Workers' International, held in Paris. His fellow-delegates from Britain were Cunninghame-Graham, and the anarchist poet, William Morris. With his usual shrewdness, Hardie attended both sections of the International, both the Marxist Congress and its more moderate 'possibilist' counterpart. Not for

B

nothing did Engels describe him as 'that super-cunning Scot'.
Hardie felt close to Marxist socialists at this time; he had met
Engels and Eleanor Marx in London as early as 1887. But soon
their revolutionary approach and their refusal to employ constitutional methods in overthrowing capitalism appeared to him im-
practical and even immoral. Hardie was never an advocate of the
class war. As he wrote in the *Labour Leader* in 1904, 'socialism
makes war upon a system, not upon a class'. He added that 'no
revolution can succeed which has not public opinion behind it. . . .
The whole thesis upon which the class war was formulated is now
antiquated and out of date.' He was later to criticize the German
socialists for rigidly adhering to Marxist formulae after the passage of time had made them largely meaningless.

In 1891 Hardie travelled abroad again, as a committee member
of the recently-formed Miners' Federation of Great Britain, to
attend the Miners' International at Jollinant in Belgium. Here he
startled the delegates by pressing for a European strike by the
miners of all countries on behalf of an immediate eight-hour day.
The internationalism of the working-class movement, political
and industrial, always appealed to Hardie. He struck up warm
friendships with labour and socialist leaders overseas, men like
August Bebel of Germany, Victor Adler of Austria, and above
all, the great French socialist leader, Jean Jaurès, whose humanitarian socialism was so similar to that of Hardie himself. Hardie
belonged to a generation for whom the nationalism of the earlier
nineteenth century, of Mazzini and Kossuth, was losing its magic,
and for whom international co-operation seemed the only alterna-
tive to war between the nations. In a real sense, a Scottish miner
in the early 1890s could feel himself to be a citizen of the world,
as Wordsworth and Burns had done during the French Revolution a century earlier.

At this time, however, Hardie's political views still appeared
imprecise. He still seemed very reluctant to call himself anything
more than an 'advanced Liberal'. The turning-point came at the
1892 general election. He had by now become utterly convinced
that a labour candidate for Parliament must above all else be truly
independent of all other parties—as the Irish Nationalists were,

and as he had himself been at Mid-Lanark in 1888. When an offer of a constituency came in South West Ham in the East End of London, Hardie jumped at the opportunity. West Ham was primarily a dockers' constituency, deeply stirred by the 'new unionism' and the dock strike of 1889. It also had a large Irish vote, more sympathetic to labour than the Irish of the Scottish coalfield. The Liberals of London were at this period alarmed at the growing threat of the working-class vote. As in 1888, they tried desperately to persuade Hardie to withdraw from the fight; but he refused to do so. Rather than risk an open clash, the Liberals withdrew themselves, giving Hardie a straight fight with his Conservative opponent, Major G. E. Banes. Not for the first or last time, Hardie based himself on a wide range of support. He stood as an anti-Conservative labour candidate, rather than the representative of a separate party. He claimed that he agreed with the Liberal Party programme 'so far as it goes'; throughout he leaned heavily on Liberal sympathies. When the result was declared, Hardie was elected by a majority of over 1,000 votes. To sustain him at Westminster (since M.P.s were not paid until 1911), the Ayrshire miners agreed to pay him a salary of £200 a year. At West Ham in 1892, a political revolution was launched. For the first time, there was an independent Labour member at Westminster, with no ties binding him to the older parties. Even though Hardie was to continue to sit in the T.U.C. until 1895, it was as a political rather than an industrial leader that he was henceforth to be known.

Hardie's election to Parliament greatly accelerated progress towards the formation of an independent socialist party. During the 1880s, a variety of organizations calling themselves socialist had come into existence. There was the Marxist Social Democratic Federation, a revolutionary body led by H. M. Hyndman, a Cambridge graduate and a former Sussex cricketer. More influential was the Fabian Society, formed in 1884. Headed by intellectuals such as Sidney and Beatrice Webb, and the playwright Bernard Shaw, it was committed to influencing the political parties by 'gradualist' methods of persuasion. Hardie himself was nominally a member of the Fabians from 1890. In the years to come, the Fabians were to have a powerful influence in the discussion of social issues. But in 1892 they, and other bodies like them, appeared to be little more than middle-class debating societies, based almost exclusively on London. Their political activity was mainly devoted to supporting Liberals or radicals in local government, especially on the newly formed London County Council, of which Sidney Webb was a notable member. Hardie and his working-class friends urged that any socialist organization must base itself firmly on the mass of the population. Further, instead of trying vainly to convert Liberals and Tories to a belief in socialism by 'gradualist' methods, a separate and independent party must be formed, based on the workers and with a distinct political creed of its own.

In many parts of the country, pressure was mounting for a new party of this kind. The main spearhead was clearly Scotland, where the Scottish Labour Party had been in existence since 1888. It still retained great prestige through Hardie's connexion with it. But it was still a small and struggling body; in the 1892 general election, its five candidates put up a disappointing showing and none reached four figures. Elsewhere in Britain, however, independent 'Labour Parties' had grown up rapidly, especially in the textile districts of Lancashire and the West Riding of Yorkshire, old strongholds of radical nonconformity. Many urged an independent party for Britain as a whole. This was advocated with especial force by the *Clarion,* probably the most effective and certainly the most readable socialist newspaper ever to appear in Britain, and edited by Robert Blatchford, an ex-soldier with a genius for popular journalism. Finally, in January 1893, an important conference was convened at Bradford, a town which boasted a wide array of Labour clubs, Labour churches, trades councils, and trade union branches. By unanimous acclaim, Hardie took the chair; the bell that he used to keep order can still be seen in the Hardie home at Cumnock as a memento of the occasion.

Here, at the Labour Institute in Bradford, came into being the Independent Labour Party, an organization without precedent, which would fight elections quite independently of all other parties. Its programme included wide measures of social reform, all apparently revolutionary then, though they have long since become law—old age pensions, national insurance, a miners' eight-hour day, the abolition of child labour, graduated income tax. This was common coin with most men of the left at this time. But the I.L.P. added a definite socialist programme, the public ownership of major industries, of land, and the means of distribution and exchange. In this sense, the I.L.P. was socialist, but its socialism was of a highly flexible kind. On Hardie's advice, the name 'Independent Labour Party' was adopted, in preference to that of 'Socialist Labour Party', which sounded more un-British. Hardie dominated the conference throughout. In 1894 he was elected first chairman of the I.L.P. and continued in office until 1899. For many years the Party remained largely his own personal instrument. In his first annual report, he claimed that it now had almost 400 branches. Significantly, the main strongholds of the I.L.P., Scotland and the West Riding, were areas where the nonconformist chapels were strong. This underlined the Party's essential character, humanitarian and idealistic, basing its appeal on comradeship and co-operation rather than on class conflict. It was attractive to men who retained a religious faith even if they had left the churches. In *After Twenty Years,* a pamphlet on the I.L.P. which he wrote in 1913, Hardie declared that 'solidarity and fraternity' were the watchwords of progress. He himself was the living symbol of its gospel, and it was fitting that he should bring the Bradford conference to a close. Quoting an old Scottish proverb, he insisted that the I.L.P. 'maun goon oor ain gate' (must go our own way). Independence was the basic principle; all else would follow. He had created for the first time in the history of English (as opposed to Irish) party politics, a third party that would take permanent root. It was among his greatest contributions to the Labour Party and the class which he fought to represent.

3

THE MAN IN THE CLOTH CAP
(1892–1900)

No new member of Parliament ever made a more flamboyant entry into the Palace of Westminster than did Keir Hardie. His West Ham constituents were determined to give their first Labour member a rousing send-off, and the results were spectacular indeed. They hired a horse-drawn wagon, with a cornet player on the box seat, to drive him from Canning Town, in dockland, to Westminster. Hardie's own attire was even more unorthodox. In place of the usual formal dress and top hat, he wore a check suit and deerstalker hat, reminiscent of Sherlock Holmes. The latter became immortalized in legend as a 'cloth cap'. It was enough to make the most conservative tremble with alarm, and wonder whether the day of red revolution was near at hand. On the other side, an extreme socialist like Hyndman wondered whether Hardie 'would live up to his cap', or whether he would succumb to the polite formalities of 'the finest debating club in the world' and lose his fire. It was as 'the man in the cloth cap' that Hardie became famous ever after.

For several years, it was hard for other members of the Commons to get used to Hardie's presence among them. With his flowing beard (always a sure symbol of revolutionary intent), his colourful dress and bright red tie, it was little wonder that Mr. Punch dubbed him 'Queer Hardie'. Westminster had never seen anything like it; even the wildest of the Irish members seemed respectably upper-class. Hardie's early ventures in the House increased the general unease felt by Liberals and Conservatives alike. From the start he was an incorrigible rebel, sitting firmly on the opposition benches, whoever was in power. His first question in the House on 18 August 1892 (on 'improving the condition of the people'), brought a pompous rebuke from the Speaker. The other 'Labour' men in the House, John Burns of Battersea, and Havelock Wilson of Middlesbrough, refused to co-operate with him, so he was a lone figure in the House. This hardly disturbed Hardie; indeed, he seemed positively to welcome his isolation. For he was appealing to the people of Britain in their slums and back-streets, not to the honourable members on the plush green benches.

It was Gladstone's last parliament, and most attention focussed on the Irish home rule bill of 1893. Hardie, however, concentrated from the outset on what seemed to him the most pressing social problem of the day, that of unemployment. In his maiden speech in February 1893, he pointed out that the Queen's Speech totally ignored the question, even though there were, he claimed, at least one million men out of work. He urged the Government to set up new public works projects, such as the reclamation of waste land, afforestation schemes, and new land cultivation; while hundreds of thousands were unemployed, the country cried out for idle labour to be put to productive use. In several later speeches, he returned to this theme. He claimed that scores of working men were actually being driven to suicide because of the grinding hardship of unemployment. Hardie's speeches were not wholly effective—his use of statistics was somewhat cavalier, while his proposed remedies were often vague. However, the facts of poverty were undeniable. A series of social surveys, notably that by Charles Booth into conditions in London, had confirmed the desperate poverty that formed the lot of the unemployed, and the lack of balance between demand and supply in an unregulated labour market. In 1895 Hardie at last made some slight impression on the Government. A Select Committee was appointed to investigate the unemployment question, while a grant of £100,000 was devoted to providing relief programmes. It was a notable triumph for a new member. Hardie himself gave evidence before the Committee. He was asked for his solution for the unemployment problem; characteristically, he replied, 'Feed them!'

In these speeches on social questions, Hardie surprised the House by the reasonable and informed nature of his approach. The member for West Ham, with his red tie and long hair, was not such a wild man after all. He was not yet at ease in the House, and unfamiliar, even impatient, with the 'shams and frivolities' of Commons' procedure. But at least he seemed to speak solid sense; further, he was learning how to make skilful use of parliamentary questions. He might even have gone through his first parliament without any serious incident, had it not been for one famous occasion in 1894. The scene he created that day was to prejudice many people against him for the rest of his career.

As an ex-miner, Hardie had been deeply moved by a serious mine disaster at the Albion Colliery in Cilfynydd in South Wales, in which 260 men had been killed. Yet the Government, in spite of all his protests, refused to find time to discuss the cause of the disaster. To show his disgust, Hardie spoke out against a motion which congratulated the Duchess of York on the birth of a son (the future King Edward VIII). Hardie was no lover of monarchy, and he said so bluntly. As the journalist A. G. Gardiner observed of him, 'he hates the palace because he remembers the pit'. Hardie declared that the country should have no use for hereditary rulers. 'It is a matter of small concern to me whether the future ruler of the nation be the genuine article or a spurious imitation.' The then Prince of Wales (later Edward VII) was no advertisement for the Crown, since he seemed to spend his time exclusively at race-courses and gambling casinos. The House of Commons had plenty of time to pass a trite motion of congratulation for the benefit of the royal family, but none to discuss 'those who are lying stark and stiff in a Welsh valley'. Hardie spoke with immense passion; all of the best and a little of the worst of him came out as he combined deep compassion for the dead miners with the puritanical scorn he felt for the waste and theatricality that surrounded the Crown. The members of Parliament were appalled, and Hardie was frequently interrupted. Harcourt, for the Liberals, and Balfour, for the Conservatives, denounced his conduct as unparliamentary and worse; Hardie's reputation as an uncouth firebrand was amply confirmed. But he himself never found cause to regret the scene he had provoked. It made him new friends in South Wales who were to serve him well later on. A succession of equally tragic mining disasters in different parts of the country seemed to confirm the moral rightness of Hardie's stand.

At the next general election, in July 1895, there was a severe reaction against the Liberal Government, and even more against extreme radicals like Hardie and his I.L.P. friends. It was the high noon of British imperialism; the electors could be swayed all too easily by patriotic appeals about painting the map of Africa and Asia with British red. Cecil Rhodes and Empire-builders like him were the popular heroes of the hour. In fact, Hardie had not spoken on foreign or imperial affairs at all during the 1892 parliament; indeed, he had not even voted on these questions, since he believed that he ought to concentrate upon social and economic questions at home. The workers ought not to be confused by foreign affairs, which, like John Bright, he regarded as a 'form of outdoor relief for the aristocracy'. However, Hardie was known to be an opponent of imperialism, and of war, which he believed was the ugly offspring of imperialism and capitalism. All this told fatally against him in the 1895 election. In addition, the Irish electors of the dockyard areas were urged by their priests not to vote for Hardie as he had attacked the Liberal Government. His only opponent, Major Banes, the Conservative he had defeated in 1892, held no meetings at all; although he was opposed to Irish home rule, Banes's son had recently become a Catholic and this attracted some Irish votes. Hardie was eventually beaten by over 800 votes, defeated, as he put it bitterly, by an unholy alliance of publicans and teetotallers, trade unionists and their 'free labour' opponents, Liberals and Tories, Irish home rulers and English imperialists, united only in their hatred of himself. The 'man in the cloth cap' was out of Parliament, and he had to begin all over again.

But his years in Parliament had served him well. He had now become the most celebrated socialist figure in the country. His appearance and accent were instantly recognizable. In the I.L.P., of which he remained chairman until 1899, he had a platform from which to propagate his views. In addition, he had now his own weekly newspaper, the *Labour Leader*, which first came out as a weekly in March 1894, and of which he was himself the major shareholder. Hardie usually wrote the editorials himself, and commented humorously on the comparatively Spartan conditions of the journal's offices. 'The floor slopes, the walls bulge but the flues draw. The bulges on the walls have been flattened and the office furniture specially designed to harmonise with the slope of the floor. If you are under 17 stone, call the first day you are in London.' The editorial staff were listed as if they were members of a family—Fred, Sam, Lily, Bob, and Bruce. There was also 'Daddy Time', who wrote the children's column 'For Lads and lasses', a pen-name which barely concealed the authorship of Hardie himself. The *Leader* was hardly the most sparkling of journals; its earnest tone seemed dull in comparison with the cheerful humanism of Blatchford's *Clarion*. Later it was to be suspect as the private vehicle of Hardie himself, occasionally used against his party colleagues, rather than the official organ of the I.L.P. But as a reliable source of information on the activities of local I.L.P. branches and on socialist movements abroad, it was immensely valuable. Sales expanded, and by 1896 it was paying its way. For the next twenty years, until it was eclipsed by the First World War, it provided the major organ of non-revolutionary socialism in Britain. Hardie's *Labour Leader* takes its place in the honoured roster of popular journals, beginning with William Cobbett's *Political Register* in the early years of the nineteenth century, which have helped on the political education of the common people.

In the *Labour Leader* and in countless pamphlets and speeches, Hardie hammered home what seemed to him the obvious moral of the 1895 election: that the workers would remain powerless as long as they were divided, and that the only possible solution was a new party to speak for labour at Westminster. The I.L.P. was too strong to disappear, but it was showing little sign of growing in most parts of the country; in London it was especially weak. Hardie again stood for Parliament in 1896, as I.L.P. candidate in a by-election in East Bradford, but he finished at the bottom of the poll with only 1,953 votes, in this socialist stronghold. By themselves, Hardie was convinced, the various socialist societies would make little headway. They had to have mass support, and this could only come from an alliance with the trade unions. The omens were now more and more favourable. The later 1890s saw trade conditions steadily deteriorating; the bubble of Victorian prosperity seemed finally to burst in the face of overseas competition. Even skilled trade unionists felt the lash of unemployment. There were lengthy strikes by the engineers in 1897 and the South Wales miners in 1898. More and more trade unionists, skilled and unskilled alike, felt that the employers were massing their forces to destroy trade unions, and were copying the tactics of the fearsome 'trusts', those combinations of firms which dominated industry in the United States, and which Hardie himself had already seen at first hand (see Chapter 6). Year after year he laboured to try to obtain the backing of the T.U.C. for a grand alliance with the socialist organizations. But it was discouraging work. When the candidature of Pete Curran of the Gasworkers in the Barnsley by-election of 1897 came to nothing because of hopeless disagreement among his supporters, even Hardie almost gave way to despair.

It was not only the trade unions that were hard to persuade; the other socialist bodies were also sceptical of the need for unity. Hyndman, of the Marxist S.D.F., never trusted Hardie; to him, Hardie was an 'opportunist' who wanted class co-operation instead of the class war preached by Marx. On the right flank, the Fabians, especially the Webbs, underestimated Hardie as they underestimated so many of their contemporaries. They despised Hardie as a crude and slow-witted working man; his vision of a labour alliance would merely bring in thousands more like him. When Hardie was defeated in the 1895 election, Beatrice Webb noted maliciously in her diary: 'Hardie has probably lost for good any chance of posturing as M.P. and will sink into the old place of a discredited Labour leader.' Yet it was Hardie's concept of a Labour alliance of socialists and trade unionists which proved more far-sighted than the Webbs' own policy of working from within the other parties. Another whose distrust Hardie aroused was the great I.L.P. editor, Robert Blatchford of the *Clarion*. Although in their different ways Hardie and Blatchford worked tirelessly for the I.L.P., they were temperamentally far apart. Hardie wrongly thought Blatchford a frivolous rake; Blatchford equally wrongly thought Hardie a puritan

and a kill-joy. Neither could ever get on terms with the other.
Blatchford, who was to survive until the coming of the Second
World War, never lost his distrust of Hardie. He wrote of him:
'He makes my flesh creep. I think he is the only man I have
ever tried to like and failed to like.'

But outside the narrow circle of socialist high politics, the
devotion Hardie inspired among ordinary working men was
now immense. His passionate, evangelical oratory was admirably
suited to the temper of an audience reared on long years of
chapel revivals. When he visited South Wales during the 1898
coal stoppage, his meetings had a messianic quality reminiscent
of nonconformist prayer meetings; only the coloured streamers
and brass bands that often greeted him showed that this was
revivalism of a secular kind. Hardie's pen also was an effective
weapon in winning converts to socialism. In the *Labour Leader*
and in a lengthy stream of popular pamphlets, he poured fourth
exposures of social injustice. Although deceptively mild and
gentle in personality, he could be hard-hitting, even bitter, in
argument. His tracts announced his message in simple compelling
terms: *Can a Man be a Christian on a Pound a Week?* was one
of the most successful. Here he argued that 'the Sermon on the
Mount is a consistent and powerful argument against property in
every form. The first great Teacher understood clearly the difference between life and a mere struggle for existence.' He also
waged a series of fierce onslaughts on Lord Overtoun, the owner
of a chemical works who was also a prominent philanthropist
and a pillar of the Church of Scotland. In Overtoun's chemical
works, Hardie showed, men worked for twelve hours a day,
seven days a week, for wages amounting to a mere 3*d.* or 4*d.*
an hour. There was a great public outcry, and conditions in
Overtoun's works rapidly improved as a result.

Hardie's endless and exhausting campaigns, however, would be
finally justified not by remedying individual cases of injustice,
important though that was, but by the forging of an alliance between the socialist societies and the trade unions. As the trade
depression worsened in the later nineties, Hardie's claims found
more and more support in the T.U.C.; in the Scottish T.U.C.,

indeed, which contained many I.L.P. members, his allies were in a majority. Finally, in 1899, the T.U.C. for the first time agreed by a narrow majority (546,000 to 434,000) to enter into negotiations with the socialist bodies to sponsor joint parliamentary candidates; Hardie himself had drafted the motion that was passed. It was an historic decision. The mounting toll of unemployment had widened dissatisfaction with the industrial system; the new mood of radical protest spurred on by the war in South Africa was to lend it further impetus. At last, Hardie's life work, the creation of a Labour Party, was near to fulfilment.

The delegates who assembled at the Memorial Hall, Farringdon Street, just off Fleet Street in London, on a rainy day in February 1900, did not look like a revolutionary assembly. Most of them were solid, bowler-hatted trade union delegates, mingling cheek by jowl with more eccentric figures such as Harry Quelch of the S.D.F. From the start, the conference was an overwhelming triumph for Keir Hardie. Instead of adopting the Fabian view of the need to 'permeate' the other parties with socialist ideas, the conference voted heavily in favour of 'a distinct labour group in Parliament', as Hardie himself urged. It was a typical Hardie compromise, a common denominator upon which almost all could agree, steering clear of theory and concentrating on the practical task on hand. It found a middle way between the intransigent approach of the S.D.F. Marxists, and the essential conservatism of the 'Lib.–Labs'.

Throughout, Hardie's skilful leadership of the conference showed that there was far more to him than empty oratory. In debates with learned Fabians, it was the simple logic of Hardie that won the day. As a result, a new Labour Representation Committee (L.R.C.) was to be formed, to which trade unions were to affiliate in growing numbers, with the object of sponsoring independent labour candidates in future elections. The executive of the L.R.C. was another Hardie compromise, with seven members from the trade unions and five from the various socialist bodies. Two of these last were from the I.L.P., one being Hardie himself; the first secretary of the L.R.C. was also an I.L.P. man,

James Ramsay MacDonald, another Scot, for whose administrative skills Hardie had a high regard. From the outset, the new body reflected the outlook of Hardie and the I.L.P., and so it remained for many years to come. At the next I.L.P. conference in Glasgow, in April 1900, Bruce Glasier paid tribute to Hardie. Even though the 'wear and tear' of propagandizing had told upon him, he had done more than any other man to build up a Labour Party. 'Yet he had never lost touch with the class to which he belonged.' Bernard Shaw once called Hardie 'the greatest natural aristocrat in the House of Commons'. As so often in his political assessments, Shaw was wide of the mark. In reality, Keir Hardie was the greatest natural democrat of them all.

4

THE MEMBER FOR MERTHYR (1900–6)

It had been generally assumed that Hardie would fight the next general election as an L.R.C. candidate, even though he was no longer to contest West Ham. Like many on the left, he was appalled by the hysteria that accompanied the South African War when it broke out in 1899. Ordinary electors could be stampeded by the patriotic fervour (or 'jingoism') of Mafeking. Soon, the British army was to be guilty of maintaining concentration camps on the Rand, in which thousands of innocent women and children were to die of disease and malnutrition. Clearly, something desperate was needed to stop the war, with all its horrors, and Hardie veered this way and that in propounding solutions. At times, he favoured a coalition of all anti-war men to restore public sanity. He appealed to the Liberal John Morley to lead such a radical alliance, but Morley, busy on his *Life* of Gladstone, was largely withdrawn from politics. This kind of coalition seemed fundamentally at variance with Hardie's continuing insistence on the need for an independent Labour Party, but he argued that the crisis of war demanded desperate remedies. One thing at least was beyond dispute. Hardie himself had to get back into Parliament without delay.

At the height of the South African War, shortly after the relief of Baden-Powell at Mafeking, the Government sprang an election on the country to try to exploit the war feeling. Hardie himself had been considering offers to stand in a number of different constituencies; eventually, he was adopted in two of them, Preston in Lancashire and Merthyr Tydfil in South Wales. (This was possible as elections then were not all fought on the same day, but spread out over a fortnight.) Hardie was told that his chances were better in Preston, and he felt certain of victory there. One of his disillusioned supporters, Sam Hobson, later reflected: 'I was now convinced that Keir Hardie had not the slightest political judgement.' In fact, the age-old tension in Lancashire politics between Irish Catholic and 'Orange' Ulsterman ruined Hardie's chances at Preston; he finished bottom of the poll, even though he obtained nearly 5,000 votes. He then rushed down to Merthyr, and in the three days left before the election made a great effort to carry the seat.

South Wales was in reality a far more fruitful territory for Hardie. Although the I.L.P. had made little headway there until the later 1890s, partly because of the barrier imposed by the Welsh language, Hardie was already widely known in the valleys. His protest on behalf of the dead miners of the Albion colliery in 1894 (see p. 24) had been widely acclaimed. In the same year, he had conducted a brief missionary campaign in South Wales. More important, Hardie had spent some time there during the six-months' coal stoppage in 1898 when 100,000 men had been thrown out of work. Hardie's compassionate articles in the *Labour Leader* made the facts of industrial distress known to a far wider public. His own personal impact upon the Welsh miners was immense. As one of them, W. J. Edwards, later reflected in *From the Valleys I Came* (1956): 'We saw him as the children of Israel must have seen Moses; a prophet showing the way through an industrial wilderness.'

Since the 1898 coal stoppage, some dramatic developments had followed in South Wales. Over thirty I.L.P. branches had been formed throughout the coalfield, while the mining trade unions, previously divided, had organized themselves into the unity of the South Wales Miners' Federation, already over 100,000 strong. Merthyr Tydfil was a natural constituency for Hardie to fight, a large two-member seat on the north-east rim of the mining valleys. It had a long tradition of radicalism, even of pacifism. This went back to the riots of 1831, when the history of the Welsh working class began and when Dic Penderyn was to go down in history as its first martyr. Merthyr had been an old centre of Chartism in the 1830s and 1840s. In the famous 1868 election, the radical nonconformist, Henry Richard, secretary of the Peace Society, had been triumphantly returned at the head of the poll. Merthyr was not only the largest and most cosmopolitan seat in Wales; it was one of the most radical and democratic constituencies in the British Isles.

But there was nothing inevitable about Hardie's victory. His supporters were divided, many of them having preferred a local Welsh miner as their candidate, instead of a Scottish outsider, however famous. The mood of the time seemed hostile to Hardie. The tide of imperialism had swept through South Wales as elsewhere, and his opponents asserted that 'a vote for Hardie was a vote for the Boers'. The I.L.P. offices in Aberdare were stoned by a mob, and Hardie's supporters assaulted. The mainstay of the Liberals, the nonconformist ministers, were almost to a man irreconcilably hostile to Hardie. Socialism, they proclaimed, was tantamount to materialism and atheism—'no government, no King, no God, absolute and impenetrable darkness'. Above all, after spending most of his time during the election in Preston, Hardie was little known in Merthyr, and his supporters found it hard going in his absence.

However, there were many factors that worked in his favour. One great advantage he enjoyed was the long rivalry between the two sitting Liberal members, D. A. Thomas and W. Pritchard Morgan. Thomas, a great coal-owner himself, disliked Morgan so intensely that he was even willing to lend indirect support to a socialist rebel like Hardie. Hardie himself was shrewd enough to spread the idea that he was appearing as Thomas's running

Hardie at his writing desk.

J. KEIR HARDIE, M.P.

KILLING NO

MURDER !

THE GOVERNMENT AND THE RAILWAY STRIKE.

What Caused the Recent Railway Strike?
Who Settled It?
For What Purpose were the Troops Called Out?

— BY —

J. KEIR HARDIE, M.P.

ONE PENNY.

THE NATIONAL LABOUR PRESS, LTD..
30. BLACKFRIARS STREET, MANCHESTER.
AND AT LONDON AND BIRMINGHAM.

Hardie's pamphlet *Killing no Murder*, 1911.

Emrys Hughes, M.P.

Emrys Hughes, M.P.

Top: Hardie (standing top right) with a group of international socialists at Lyons, 1912. Jean Jaurès writing.
Above: Hardie with a group of M.P.s on the terrace of the House of Commons, 1912.

Top: Hardie speaking at an anti-war demonstration, 2 August 1914.
Above: Keir Hardie and his wife at Caterham, 1914.

mate, however unlikely the partnership. Again, if imperialism was strong in Merthyr, so too was anti-imperialism. After all, it was only a generation since the Merthyr Boroughs had elected Henry Richard, the apostle of peace. Many Welsh people felt that the English Government was acting as a bully in waging war upon the Boers, a small, Protestant, farming community—rather like Wales itself, in fact. Lloyd George benefited from this feeling in Caernarvon Boroughs, and so did Hardie in Merthyr. Finally, the old tradition of working-class co-operation, dating from the earliest years of industrialism in the late eighteenth century, was still very much alive. As a result, amid immense excitement, Hardie was returned as the second member, defeating Pritchard Morgan by over 1,700 votes. He won mainly through receiving second votes from D. A. Thomas's supporters. But he was back in Parliament, never to lose Merthyr again.

For the rest of his career, Hardie was closely identified with Welsh life; the loyal devotion of his Welsh supporters proved unflinching. As the first independent Labour member for Wales, Hardie had introduced a totally new element into Welsh politics, dominated for so long by the Liberal Party and the chapels. Yet he soon felt very much at home. He joined the Welsh parliamentary party, and acted with Liberal colleagues in supporting such national Welsh demands as disestablishment of the Church of England in Wales. He even supported a form of Welsh home rule. He claimed to be a Welsh nationalist; indeed, Labour was the only nationalist party, since it alone wanted the land of Wales to belong to its people. 'The red dragon and the red flag' provided a slogan for his new journal, the *Merthyr Pioneer* : it recognized that the doctrines of socialism must be adapted to a local Welsh setting. He even learnt to sing the Welsh national anthem, the unfamiliar words of '*Hen wlad fy nhadau*' ringing out in a rich Scots baritone. He liked the Welsh: 'like all true Celts, they are socialists by instinct'. In his later years he was to become more and more remote from Merthyr, as his travels took him to many distant parts of the world. But his hold over the affections of his growing army of faithful Welsh supporters stood secure.

Now that Hardie was back in Parliament, however, he had

c

also to find a base in London. Life was still hard for him. It was assumed that members of Parliament would have a substantial private income; Hardie, of course, had none. His sole property was the 'mansion', the solid house he had at Cumnock. He was largely dependent on the £150 that he received annually from the Ayrshire Miners' Union. After some difficulty, he found rooms in London in a secluded court of Queen Anne buildings, Nevill's Court, just off Fleet Street (later to be destroyed by German bombs in 1941). Here, Hardie received socialist leaders from Britain and from many other countries. His dress, as recalled by the young Fenner (later Lord) Brockway, was simple, usually a tweed suit, with an open-necked shirt. Smoking heavily through an ancient pipe, he would reflect on how he had become a socialist himself twenty years ago. He seemed already a veteran of the movement, even though he was still only in his middle forties. It was a Spartan life he lived there. On an income of £3 a week, he and his wife had to pay £1 in food, 15s. for secretarial help, and a further 6s. in rent. In addition, there were frequent long railway journeys to his Merthyr constituency, or home to Scotland. Guests of his at the Commons expected to be entertained to tea on the terrace, and this made further inroads into his income. To make ends meet, he had to write for the Press, or else take on additional paid week-end meetings. In spite of the continuing harshness of life, however, he retained his compassion and his sense of humour. One day, a policeman saw Hardie entering the lobby of the Commons. Not recognizing the strangely clad new member, he asked him, 'Do you work here, mate?' Hardie replied that he did. 'Where, on the roof?' asked the policeman. 'No,' replied Hardie, 'on the floor.'

He was soon back in action in debates, speaking on a host of topics from the rights and wrongs of the war in South Africa to the torture of albatrosses on passenger vessels bound for Australia. He was still quite literally a colourful member. The *Daily News* reporter noted that 'his tie still blushes a vivid red'. His strange hat was a souvenir from Philadelphia. He was still contemptuous of many of the medieval trappings of Parliament, though he noted that the new dining-room, smoking-room, and baths, and improvements to the terraces made the Commons much more comfortable than it had been in 1895. He felt much more at home in the House now, especially when a series of by-elections in 1902 and 1903 returned some more Labour members to join him. His speeches were more relaxed than before, while his more moderate tone won him a more sympathetic hearing, especially from radicals like Lloyd George. He was less out to shock, more to convince. He was learning that the best way to bring about the socialist revolution was by persuasion and consent.

His return to the House was marked by a series of fierce speeches denouncing the Boer War in general, and the Colonial Secretary, Joseph Chamberlain, in particular. He alleged that the war had been started to boost the profits of finance houses and arms manufacturers. Chamberlain himself was involved in the munitions industry; as Lloyd George wittily put it, 'As the Empire expands, the Chamberlains contract.' Hardie's line of attack found ready support from radical 'pro-Boers' and Irish Nationalists with whom he sat below the gangway. Lloyd George in particular aroused Hardie's admiration. In an open letter in the *Labour Leader,* Hardie appealed to him to found a new anti-imperialist, social reform party, but in vain. Hardie also turned once more to his familiar theme of denouncing wasteful expenditure on the royal family. He attacked the pomp and circumstance that surrounded the funeral of Queen Victoria in 1901. 'The dead body of the Queen was being used as a recruiting sergeant.' However, this line of argument was not calculated to broaden his support. Hardie's most constructive speeches were on subjects such as unemployment, old age pensions, and school meals for children. He helped persuade the Conservative Government to pass the Unemployed Workmen Act, a moderate reform introduced in 1905. He also encouraged those younger Liberals, like Lloyd George, who sought a 'new Liberalism' of social reform. To Hardie, however, social reform was not an end in itself but the first stage only towards a socialist commonwealth.

One topic on which Hardie spoke out with especial vehemence was the 1905 Aliens Bill. In those days, Labour members were bitterly opposed to the restriction of the free entry of immigrants into Britain, and Hardie himself was particularly emphatic. He argued that Britain's duty was to provide a safe refuge for poor, homeless people such as the Jews who were fleeing from mass slaughter in the Russian 'pogroms'. To tighten up restrictions by deportation orders would put a dangerous weapon in the hands of Government which could easily be abused. Hardie and his friends believed almost literally in the brotherhood of man. They extended the hand of comradeship equally to English and Welsh, Scots and Irish, Jews and Gentiles, Indians and South African 'kaffirs'. They could not foresee that, sixty years later, a Labour Government and a Labour Home Secretary would curtail so drastically the immigration of coloured people into Britain.

Hardie greatly increased his prestige in the House on this and other issues. But, despite all his efforts, the independent L.R.C. members in the House numbered a mere handful of four or five. The ideal of a national Labour Party was still very far from being fulfilled. The L.R.C. had no national organization, and was really little more than a loose federation of different organizations, some industrial and some political, up and down the country. It would take many years of struggle to achieve the socialist utopia, and Hardie knew it. Every year, he spoke at the annual conferences of the L.R.C. and the I.L.P., and at countless similar gatherings, urging patience on the members. The immediate need, as he saw it, was to establish a firm parliamentary foothold, without which the L.R.C. would be impotent. But it was very difficult for such a comparatively poor body to obtain one, all by itself. The only possible answer was some kind of electoral pact with the Liberals, the likely winners of the next election and the more radical of the two major parties. Some kind of arrangement must be made which would prevent Labour and Liberal candidates fighting each other at by-elections and general elections. On the other hand, any agreement reached must not compromise Labour's essential independence; Labour must be equal partners in the pact, not satellites or hangers-on. This was in many ways an unpopular line to advocate. Many people found genuine difficulty in understanding what Hardie meant by the 'independence' of Labour, especially since he co-operated so readily with Liberals in the House. Was Labour intended to be a separate political party, or just a vague pressure-group of left-wing Liberals? To more extreme socialists, such as Hyndman, Hardie's approach merely confirmed him as a shallow man, without political judgement.

The outcome of Hardie's pressure was a secret pact concluded in February 1903 between Ramsay MacDonald for the L.R.C. and the Liberal Chief Whip, Herbert Gladstone. MacDonald was in touch with Hardie throughout. The result was that Labour candidates would be free of Liberal opposition in about thirty seats in the next election. Liberals would save the money and trouble of fighting Labour here, while Labour would have an agreed quota of seats in which it would have a free run against the Conservatives. This agreement was carried out surprisingly faithfully in the next election. Without it, Labour would have had immense difficulty in ever establishing itself as a third force in politics. The future was to show that the Liberals had miscalculated badly; it was Labour who really benefited by the 1903 pact. From this time really begins the process by which Labour supplanted the Liberals as the leading party of the left.

When the next election came in January 1906, everything was in Labour's favour. There was obviously going to be a Liberal victory, though in those days without Gallup polls it was not possible to gauge its magnitude. The outgoing Balfour Government had been divided and discredited. Its attack on free trade seemed to most people to mean a 'dear loaf' and a huge increase in the cost of living. Further, nonconformists, the spearhead of Liberalism still, had been bitterly antagonized by the 1902 Education Act, which, it was claimed, would 'put Rome on the rates' by publicly subsidizing Church schools. More important, working men had been appalled by the Taff Vale case in 1901, in which the right to strike had been undermined. A railway union had been forced to pay £23,000 to the company after a strike on the Taff Vale Railway. In future, it appeared, trade unions would be liable to pay huge damages if they were engaged in labour disputes. For all these reasons, working-class electors turned violently against the Conservatives. The only reply they could offer was the 'patriotic' appeal of imperialism. But the high noon of Empire was passing; the glory of the South African War had turned sour amid the horrors of Kitchener's concentration camps. A new concern with social problems was taking its place. At the election, therefore, the unfortunate Conservatives were swamped. They retained a mere 157 members, as against 401 Liberals and a further 86 Irish Nationalists. The defeat of the Conservatives, the worst ever in their history, was humiliating and complete.

The most spectacular result of the election, however, was the return of twenty-nine Labour members under the auspices of the L.R.C. The 1903 pact brought its rich reward. Hardie himself was one of the twenty-nine. He himself had fought a vigorous campaign. Two years earlier, his health, always suspect, had given way completely. He was much weakened by an operation for appendicitis (a much more dangerous illness then than it is now), and he had to give up work entirely for a while. In addition, he was deeply saddened by the deaths, in rapid succession, of his mother and stepfather in 1902. He was also distressed by party disagreements which forced him to yield control of the *Labour Leader* in 1904. But his reserves of courage and determination rescued him soon enough from despair. By January 1906 he was back in the fray, campaigning hard from London to Newcastle-upon-Tyne. He neglected Merthyr almost entirely, and his supporters there had to work hard to beat off the challenge of a last-minute Liberal opponent, Henry Radcliffe, a shipowner. Hardie's programme was as radical as ever—nationalization of major industries, votes for women, home rule for Wales, Scotland and Ireland, abolition of the House of Lords, a severe cut in spending on the armed forces. In the event, he won by a comfortable margin of nearly 3,000 votes. He returned to Westminster in triumph to meet his new Labour colleagues. In the House, they formed themselves into a new group, the Parliamentary Labour Party. The currents of idealism were surging through the new radical Parliament of 1906. At last, it seemed that the new Jerusalem would be built in England's green and pleasant land.

5

THE PARTY LEADER (1906–14)

THE new Parliament of 1906 marked a turning-point in the life of Keir Hardie. He had made his name as a pioneer. His career symbolized the struggle of labour to obtain a first foothold in politics. That had now been attained. Now that there was a Labour Party in existence, Hardie had to adapt himself to the problems of power and influence. The transition was not easy to make.

His reputation in the labour movement was still immense. He was still the best-known and best-loved of all Labour leaders, instantly recognizable with his beard, his red tie, his slouch hat, and his Inverness cloak. But physically he was no longer the man he once had been. Years of poor health and of exhausting campaigns had left their mark. The strain had been intense. In one week in 1894, for instance, he had journeyed to Dundee, Leeds, Bradford, Halifax, and Bolton, addressed meetings in the East End of London, conducted his editorial duties in the *Labour Leader* offices, and twice paid visits to the Commons. It was more than any man could stand. Although now only fifty years of age, he was already wrinkled and white-haired, his brow scored with deep furrows. He looked at least twenty years older, already a veteran of the movement. Increasingly, it was a younger genera-tion of socialists, men like Ramsay MacDonald and Philip Snow-den, who were stealing the limelight. Hardie had already lost control of the *Labour Leader*, and disagreements over the finan-cial settlement due to him still rankled. Ramsay MacDonald com-plained that it was dull reading. More fundamentally, he thought it was an organ for putting across Hardie's own views, which were sometimes contrary to those of the I.L.P. leadership. To the last, Hardie was essentially an individualist, and an erratic Party man.

When the election was held for the first chairmanship of the new Parliamentary Labour Party in the 1906 session of Parliament, several trade union representatives opposed Hardie's nomination and preferred the cautious Lancashire weaver, David Shackleton. Hardie was elected by a majority of one vote only. Even in this year of electoral triumph, the future internal divisions of the Labour Party were foreshadowed.

As chairman of the Parliamentary Party, Hardie was only a partial success. He found the discipline of leadership irksome, and left Arthur Henderson to discuss arrangements for the order of business in the House. Eventually, Hardie resigned at the end of 1908 to pursue his own course. His formal speeches on behalf of his party in the House were not successful; they tended to be rambling and tedious. He remained a prophet rather than a parliamentarian. He completely lacked the sympathy with the mood of the Commons later to be shown by MacDonald. He and MacDonald, in fact, found themselves more and more at odds in the years up to 1914; perhaps in part it was a difference of temperament between the lowland Scot and the Highlander. Hardie distrusted MacDonald's liking for London society; he suspected that MacDonald might betray Labour's hard-won independence in a deal with the Liberals. However, the occasion in 1931 when MacDonald was to split his party and to form a 'National Government' with the Conservatives lay far in the future.

It may, however, be doubted whether Hardie was as ineffective a Party leader as some historians have claimed. He had still vital work to do in directing the young, fractious Labour Party along constitutional lines. In the country, he was still among the most formidable of platform orators, even when he came near to being physically assaulted during a stormy visit to Cambridge University in 1907. His speech on that occasion converted a young undergraduate called Hugh Dalton to socialism on the spot. In the House, the Labour Party had some great triumphs under his chairmanship; notable among these was the passage of Labour's Trades Disputes Bill in 1906 which reversed the Taff Vale decision. Some of Hardie's speeches were still very effective, particularly when he dealt with unemployment and other social problems which he knew at first hand. He attacked the Government for neglect of the unemployment problem: over two million were now out of work. Soon, Winston Churchill as Home Secretary, was to begin a totally new chapter in social policy by setting up labour exchanges to regulate the supply and demand for labour; while in 1911 Lloyd George's great scheme for social insurance marked a decisive landmark in the foundation of the welfare state.

Hardie's speeches were invariably passionate and intense. Yet this was often misleading. His essential approach was moderate. One question that showed this up clearly was that of women's suffrage. He was foremost among M.P.s who urged that women should be granted the vote as a basic political right. But he always insisted that women's suffrage must come gradually; at first they must be content with the same limited franchise as men. It was unreasonable to demand, as many 'suffragettes' did, that all women over twenty-one should be given the vote at once; public opinion was not ready for this. For this cautious approach, Hardie occasionally found himself in the ironic position of being himself heckled at meetings by suffragettes. Many of them were now bent on violent action, breaking windows, slashing paintings in art galleries, dropping bombs in pillar boxes—anything to draw attention to their grievances. One suffragette even threw herself in front of the King's horse during the Derby at Epsom. To extremists such as these, and their sympathizers in the Labour Party like George Lansbury, Hardie's gradualism was far too slow. At the annual conference of the Labour Party at Belfast in March 1907, a motion was overwhelmingly carried demanding that the parliamentary party should advocate complete suffrage for all adult men and women immediately. Hardie announced that if the conference meant to tie the hands of the parliamentary party by this resolution, he would resign. This caused a sensation, but Hardie's view of the '1907 formula' has largely governed the future internal development of the Labour Party. In later years, Attlee, Gaitskell, and Wilson all adopted the same view as Hardie; to have the annual conference dictating policy to the parliamentary party would be highly undemocratic. On this and other occasions, Hardie's personal authority helped to keep the Party to the moderate line. However, when the Liberal Government mal-treated suffragette prisoners and resorted to forcible feeding, Hardie was the first to condemn these degrading methods.

During this period, in Britain, Germany, France, and many other countries, there was taking place a great debate about basic socialist principles. Fundamentally, it concerned whether Marx's analysis of the character of industrial society was as relevant in 1900 as it had been in the 1840s and 1850s. Was it really true, as Marx had claimed, that the gulf between classes was growing ever wider, that the workers were becoming poorer and more repressed, and that the capitalist system was on the point of imminent collapse through its own inherent contradictions? Hardie made his own contribution to this debate in one of his very few books, *From Serfdom to Socialism,* published in 1907. Here he outlined his vision of socialism. It was, he argued, much more than a political creed or an economic dogma. Basically, it was ethical, an ideal of a better, fuller, and happier life for everyone, no matter to which class he belonged. It was a doctrine of love, not of hatred, very close in principle to the Sermon on the Mount. Hardie thought there had been a time when conditions of life had been much more secure for the common people; the fifteenth century had been 'the golden age of the English worker'. But over the centuries, capitalism had transformed society; while trusts and combines sucked away the wealth of the nation, half of the workers earned less than a meagre £1 a week. The only remedy was socialism—but it could only come gradually, by persuasion, in local and central government. Socialism would not crush the individual; it would give him a far more satisfying life. It would base itself on the working class, yet the support of middle-class allies should also be welcomed. Socialism offered to wealthy men the joy of useful service; it could not be based on the poor alone—'it is the slum vote which the socialist candidate fears most'. Hardie followed up his book with a further stream of pamphlets on these themes, on the meaning of socialism and the tactics to be pursued in bringing it about. The most famous of these was *My Confession of Faith in the Labour Alliance,* written in 1909. Here he saw the Labour Party not as a narrow sect but as a broad alliance, ranging from Marxists to trade unionists, representative of the nation as a whole. Labour's main need was for tolerance; extremist splinter groups operating on the flanks would be powerless. Labour's creed was never a rigid one, and it should welcome support, from whatever class it came, from all who would work for socialism.

Hardie's views undoubtedly summed up the attitude of the great mass of Labour supporters. But then, as so often since, there were many who were impatient with this apparently un-heroic caution. They saw Hardie, MacDonald, and all the parliamentary party in the same light as all the other M.P.s, cor-rupted by the club-like atmosphere of the Commons. For the first time since 1893, Hardie's own leadership of the I.L.P. came under fire—and the I.L.P. was still the most influential socialist body in the country. The protest within its ranks found its symbol in Victor Grayson, an angry and unstable young man who had been returned to Parliament in a famous by-election in Colne Valley in 1907. He seemed to embody the spirit of youthful revolt. The I.L.P., he claimed, had ceased to be socialist, since it no longer sought a revolution; it had been corrupted by alliance with conservative trade unionists and Fabians. In the Commons, Grayson refused to sign the constitution of the Labour Party and went his own way. He found a ready ally in Hardie's old enemy, Blatchford, anxious for any stick with which to belabour Hardie's puritanism and pacifism. Finally, in the annual I.L.P. conference at Edinburgh in 1909, Grayson's supporters carried a motion concerning affiliation to the Labour Party, against the advice of the executive. In protest, Hardie, MacDonald, Snowden, and Glasier, the four most influential figures in the Party, promptly resigned from the executive. This achieved its effect. Grayson's reputation never recovered; in any case, he was defeated at the next general election. Later he mysteriously disappeared and was never seen again. The I.L.P. soon recovered from these internal differences and regained much of its old authority. Not until the 1918 Labour Party constitution created a nation-wide party organization on a constituency basis, three years after Hardie's death, did the I.L.P. enter upon its final decline.

Hardie's own position in the I.L.P. was promptly restored, and he was re-elected to the Executive in 1911. The annual conference of the Party was held in Merthyr in 1912, as a personal tribute to him. Finally, he served again as chairman at the twenty-first Party conference in 1914, which marked the Party's coming-of-age. It was an emotional moment. At the final rally in St. George's Hall, Bradford, the scene of the first I.L.P. conference in 1893, Hardie suddenly turned away from the audience and addressed instead the children assembled on the stage behind him. He appealed to them to love flowers, to love animals, to love their fellows, to hate injustice and cruelty, never to be mean or treacherous, always to be generous in service. He told them how unnecessary were poverty and war, and how he had tried to pass on a world where happiness and peace would be theirs. He and those who had worked with him had failed, but they, the children, would succeed. He made a final emotional appeal: 'If these were my last words, I would say them to you, lads and lasses. Live for that better day!' Soon afterwards, the First World War broke out, which seemed to destroy all his hopes. But the simple faith of his appeal lived on.

As a prophetic figure, Hardie's authority was still unrivalled. But in the day-to-day turmoil of politics, he felt more and more ill at ease. He was intensely unhappy at the course followed by the Labour Party since he resigned his chairmanship in 1908. As an independent Party it seemed to count for very little. Hardie defended in the *Socialist Review* and other journals the decision to support Lloyd George's 'People's Budget' of 1909, which the Lords rejected. Hardie claimed that it would help on the socialist cause. But privately, to Bruce Glasier, he spoke of his dismay at the Party's lack of independence. In the Commons, it often cut a pitiable figure. In the debates on the National Insurance Bill of 1911, for instance, Labour members voted on opposite sides, and no clear Labour policy emerged at all. Hardie was now on bad terms with the new chairman of the Parliamentary Party, MacDonald. He suspected him of being a careerist, while Hardie also subscribed fully to the traditional Labour suspicion of 'leaders' as a class. He feared that MacDonald contemplated an open alliance with the Liberals in the coming election of 1915, and he tried to persuade Snowden, Henderson, and others to turn against their leader. MacDonald, for his part, complained of Hardie's 'unfortunate way of doing things ... He is determined to regard himself as a freelance when it suits him, and as a member of a team when it suits him.' He pointed out, with some justice, that Hardie himself had strongly approved the pact with the Liberals in 1903; yet now he considered such an alliance highly dangerous. The dispute continued to rankle, and not until the outbreak of the First World War were cordial relations restored between the two Scottish Labour leaders.

Hardie's dismay at the course being followed by the Labour Party was much intensified by the tumultuous wave of industrial unrest in the period 1910–14. It was a time of extraordinary violence—the suffragettes, the Irish Unionists, diehards in the House of Lords, workers on strike in basic industries, all seemed to have burst the bonds of restraint, and to be turning to a violent solution of their demands. No part of the United Kingdom was more turbulent than Hardie's own South Wales. From 1908 onwards, there was a series of long and savage strikes in the mining valleys, culminating in the frightening riots at Tonypandy in November 1910. Here, one miner was killed, and the Home Secretary, Winston Churchill, was forced to send troops in to protect law and order—an action which was remembered and resented in the valleys for decades to come. The whole coalfield seemed to be seething with a strange new turbulence. A new young generation of miners' leaders demanded an end to industrial harmony and to conciliation with the owners. *The Miners' Next Step,* a pamphlet published at Tonypandy in 1912, urged that the miners should take 'direct action' to bring the whole system of private ownership crashing down in ruins. The workers should form councils to run mines and factories themselves, for their own benefit, not for the profits of capitalist owners. Feeling was further inflamed by a series of appalling mining accidents, culminating in the Senghenydd pit disaster in 1913

when over 400 miners lost their lives. Like Clydeside and the
London docks, the South Wales coalfield seemed to have become
the battlefield for the class war between masters and men.

Keir Hardie was deeply distressed by all these developments.
He was passionately stirred by some of the methods used by
the police to restore order. In a series of debates in the Commons
in 1910–11, he attacked Churchill for failing to investigate proven
cases of police brutality. He wrote a searing tract, *Killing no
Murder,* when troops shot down and killed two railwaymen
during a strike in Llanelli in 1911. But, basically, Hardie felt out
of sympathy with the new disturbances. However justifiable they
might be, the men were using the wrong weapons. He himself
was, above all else, a man of peace. He deplored the formation
of 'fighting brigades' of miners, and the bloodthirsty speeches of
some miners' leaders, some of whom were to denounce the 'Huns'
as violently in 1914 as they did the owners now. Hardie criticized
the tactics of the authors of the *Miners' Next Step* (some of whom
were to join the Communist Party after 1918). In an American
magazine, the *Metropolitan,* Hardie explained that while the
miners were right to demand a minimum wage (in fact, this was
passed by Parliament in 1913), they were wrong to substitute a
strike for political action. The miners should trust the state, not
destroy it. They should use the state for their own ends, through
a Labour Party, instead of turning to the mirage of 'workers'
control'. They should believe in orderly progress, rather than
urge a class war. But in the heady days of 1913 and 1914, it was
difficult to hear Hardie's counsel of peace. The class struggle
that Marx had prophesied really seemed to be at hand.

On the whole, the progress of the Labour Party between 1906
and 1914 had been disappointing. The twenty-nine members of
the parliamentary party in 1906 had risen to only forty, and this
increase was due entirely to the affiliation of the miners' members.
There was no sign of a new advance. The party seemed ineffective
compared with the Liberals, and deeply divided within itself.
There were clashes of personality over the leadership. Even more,
there was dissension over basic political principles. Did the future
really lie in violent industrial agitation, or in gradual constitu-

tional pressure at Westminster? Was the Labour Party really a national party at all, or just a loose federation of pressure groups? And what, if anything, did the Labour Party stand for? Some of its members were socialists of various kinds; most were not and were hardly distinguishable from the Liberals. No clear answers seemed to emerge.

Yet, in retrospect, the period 1906–14 is seen to be crucial in the evolution of the Party. In spite of all discouragement, it had established a base from which it could not easily be driven out. The adherence of the miners in 1909 meant that there was now a hard core of thirty to forty seats which Labour was bound to retain. Here, it was Liberalism that was on the retreat. Further, the Trade Union Act of 1913 had given legal guarantees to the Labour Party's funds by sanctioning the political levy from trade unions. Hardie himself had campaigned hard against the Osborne Judgement of 1908 which had invalidated political contributions from trade unions. Above all, in the difficult years up to 1914, Labour held firm to the parliamentary method, and for this Hardie himself must take a good deal of the credit. By argument and by example, he urged year after year the need for moderation, and for making Labour a national party representative of the whole community, rather than just the defensive pressure-group of a single class. He fought hard against those who preferred a narrow sect to a mass party, and even more those who advocated the path of violence and revolution. Just as he had been the architect of the Party before 1906, so in large measure he was to be one of its saviours in the years that followed.

6

THE INTERNATIONALIST

As he grew older, Hardie's horizon extended far beyond the British scene. He had always been an internationalist, and an apostle of the ideal of the brotherhood of man. He had urged the breaking down of national barriers between the four nations of the United Kingdom itself. After 1900, Hardie's internationalism became a more and more integral part of his socialism. Perhaps, indeed, his major contribution to the labour movement in these later years lay less in his work at home, and more in the links he helped to forge with socialist bodies in many different countries throughout the world.

Since the later 1880s, he had been in close touch with socialist and working-class movements on the continent of Europe. He travelled widely from the 1890s onwards to European socialist congresses, either as 'fraternal delegate' from Britain or simply as an observer. Hardie thought there was much to learn from socialist comrades on the Continent—perhaps something to avoid also. The German Social Democrats (S.P.D.) illustrated for him the difficulty of reconciling Marxist dogma with day-to-day parliamentary tactics. The French socialists showed the fatal effects of internal disunity; Jaurès, thought Hardie, made far too many concessions to his extremists, the French counterparts of Grayson and Hyndman. In France, also, the progress of socialism had been slowed down by anti-clerical attacks on the Churches, which Hardie condemned. However, he always thought it a vital matter to preserve links with his European comrades. Certainly, he would have been surprised to find how insular the Labour Party became after his death.

Hardie was also a very active member of the various congresses of the Socialist International, that assembly of socialist organizations from different countries that met in various cities in Europe between 1889 and 1912. But he was not an internationalist here in the sense of German revolutionaries like Rosa Luxemburg; he was always on the side of those who urged moderation. In the 1904 Amsterdam Congress, he backed up the French Socialists after Millerand, one of their leading members, had joined a 'bourgeois' radical government. After all, Millerand's action was little different from the 'Lib.–Lab.' pact of 1903 in Britain. One issue that Hardie made his own at congresses of the International was that of a general strike against war. As we shall shortly see (Chapter 7), he was deeply concerned at the rise of the military spirit in Europe. At the Copenhagen Congress of the International in 1910, he urged a strike by all the socialist parties in Europe if war should come. But he tended to be imprecise on exactly how this would be effected, while other Europeans rejected his views. The Frenchman, Jaurès, demanded a citizen's militia, while the Germans, led by Bebel, insisted that Germany must maintain an army to deal with the threat from Russia. In practice, then, the Socialist International was neither as socialist nor as internationalist as Hardie hoped and believed.

Hardie's internationalism was very far from being confined to Europe alone. He made also three visits to the United States, in 1895, 1908, and 1912. While many British socialists then and since have distrusted America as being supposedly dominated by big business and 'Wall Street', for Hardie's generation the United States was still a hopeful and progressive country, with a revolutionary past. In 1895, the year of Hardie's first visit, there were radical protest movements throughout the United States, especially by the Populist Party in the agrarian West and South. Hardie spent fifteen weeks there, in the company of his friend, Frank Smith, a member of the Salvation Army. They visited New York to meet Daniel de Leon and other American socialist leaders. In a gaol near Chicago, they met perhaps the most famous of all American socialists, Eugene V. Debs, who had been imprisoned for his part in organizing the American Railway Union. Characteristically, Debs's main memory of Hardie was of a gentle man, who took the trouble to transfer a locust trapped in a bottle to a cigar-box he had filled with grass. Hardie went on across the Middle West and great plains to the mining areas of the North-West, where an impromptu solo by a Scottish piper in Butte, Montana, paid for his expenses at a time when he and Smith were almost penniless. In San Francisco, Hardie was offered a gift of £20,000 to the I.L.P. if he would come out in favour of a currency based on silver instead of gold. This was cheerfully added to the long list of 'bribes I have been offered'. Hardie came back much excited by what he had seen, and kept up close links with his American comrades.

In 1908, he paid a briefer visit. In the presidential election of

D

that year, the socialist vote (for Debs) was a poor one. Hardie saw that, as in Britain, the main need was for an alliance between Debs's American Socialist Party and the trade unions. But American unions were opposed to political action, still more to socialism. Their leader, Sam Gompers, also a friend of Hardie's, asked bluntly: 'What does Labour want? More!!' Hardie thought that a new Labour Party might be based on the silver, copper, and lead miners of the far North-West, Montana, Idaho, and Oregon, a community so similar to the mining villages of Wales and Scotland that he knew so well. In his final visit in 1912, Hardie thought his optimism fully justified, since Debs polled almost a million votes in the presidential election. Milwaukee elected Victor Berger, the first Socialist ever returned to Congress. But events since were to make Hardie's visions of a Socialist America seem illusory. Perhaps he failed to see some of the essential differences between British and American working men. In fact, there were profound regional and ethnic divisions that prevented the American workers from forming a nation-wide party, while they tended to see themselves as independent producers in a land of opportunity, rather than as members of a labouring class bound down by the wage system. At least, however, Hardie had a positive view of Anglo-American co-operation, instead of the sterile anti-Americanism which has so often marked the British—and even more the British right.

Hardie's most spectacular travels came in 1907 when, after a further bout of illness, he went on a trip round the world. His expenses were met by the I.L.P. and the Quakers. At first, he sailed again westwards across the Atlantic, to Canada. He liked the freshness and vitality of Canada, but pointed out that unemployment was as high there as in Britain itself. Emigration from Britain to the white dominions was no answer to the country's economic problems.

Then he sailed on across the Pacific to the sub-continent of India. In 1907, India was seething with nationalist unrest, especially in Bengal, while a severe famine had led to the death of tens of thousands of peasants. Hardie was much moved by what he saw, and described his impressions in a small book, *India:*

Impressions and Suggestions (1909). He outlined the sad facts of Indian poverty. While millions were starving, 75 per cent of the revenue from harvests went in taxes. The average annual income of the Indian peasant was a mere 26s.—in Britain the average was £42. Famine and pestilence were rife. The Indian system of government was equally deplorable. The British had broken up the old system, and had partitioned Bengal against all the wishes of its people. The Government of India was little more than a vast military despotism. Hardie also noted the existence of a 'colour bar' with British 'pukka sahibs' and their wives scarcely treating the ordinary Indian Hindu or Moslem as a human being. It was not surprising that during his tour Hardie addressed huge nationalist demonstrations in Bengal, accompanied by leaders of the Congress movement. He alleged that British atrocities in India were as bad as those of the Turks in Armenia. The answer was that India should have self-government just like Canada and Australia.

This caused an immense uproar in Britain. India was the richest jewel of the old Empire, romanticised by Rudyard Kipling. *The Times* raged against the 'criminal ignorance and criminal recklessness' of Hardie's speeches, and urged the Viceroy to have him deported. Hardie was denounced generally in the British Press; in vain did he complain that he had been misreported. The fact remained that for the first time, a visiting politician had viewed Indian society from the standpoint of the Indians, not that of British Raj. In 1907 Hardie was abused and ridiculed; forty years later, India was given independence, much as he had fore-told.

Unscathed by his troubles in India, Hardie continued his Asian tour. He visited the Straits Settlement (now Malaysia and Singapore), and Japan, where he roundly condemned the persecution of Japanese socialists by the Emperor. Then he went south to Australia, where his reception was much warmer. The Australian Labour Party was now firmly established, and Hardie was welcomed by old associates such as Andrew Fisher of the Ayrshire Miners' Union, and H. H. Champion, who had been his election agent in Mid-Lanark back in 1888. Hardie played cricket for the

Australian Parliament against the Press, and recorded with pride that he scored eight runs, including a boundary. Here, and later in New Zealand, he was impressed by the absence of class distinction, compared with the Old World. The nationalized coal-mines of New Zealand were a heartening example of state enterprise in practice. Hardie greatly enjoyed Australasia, though later the military spirit of the Australian Labour Party, under the Welshman 'Billy' Hughes, was to distress him.

Finally, his world tour took him to South Africa. This proved the most turbulent part of his travels. He outraged the Boer farmers, whom he had himself championed so courageously during the recent war, by suggesting that coloured workers be given social and political rights. This aroused all the racial prejudice of the South African Dutch, and Hardie was bitterly attacked as a 'nigger lover'. His final meeting at Johannesburg almost provoked a riot. He escaped with a tattered Union Jack which he later kept as a trophy at Nevill's Court. Here again Hardie anticipated the future. He foresaw that the independence of the Union of South Africa left the position of the coloured majority quite untouched.

Hardie's return to Britain was enthusiastically acclaimed by the Labour Party. He had added a new dimension to its programme by committing it firmly to colonial self-government and racial equality. Hardie's tour also affected his own career. Hitherto, he had been largely identified with domestic politics. Now he was to make a series of striking and well-informed speeches in the House on India and South Africa. In speeches on the India budget from 1908 onwards, he underlined the poverty and misgovernment of India, the need for expanded programmes of educational and agrarian reform, the evils of the 'colour bar', and the urgency of associating Indians with the government of their own country. All this sounds commonplace today; in 1908, it seemed treasonable. In debates on the Union of South Africa Bill in 1910, Hardie was almost alone in raising the question of the coloured population, and their lack of any political power. Riots by coloured workers in Cape Colony emphasized the grievances he had noted, but the Government ignored the problem. Here, and in so much else, Hardie showed himself truly prophetic. He could detect, in 1910, the 'wind of change' of African and Asian nationalism that Harold Macmillan was to describe so eloquently fifty years later. Hardie's other contacts with overseas nationalism were astonishingly wide. In 1909 he travelled to Geneva to meet exiled members of the Young Egypt party, and advised them to follow the constitutional path in pushing for self-government: the Wafd Party was to follow his advice after 1918. Hardie made an immense contribution to the discussion of colonial and racial questions; his legacy is writ large on the world of the later twentieth century.

7

THE MAN OF PEACE (1914–15)

THROUGHOUT his career, Keir Hardie had been above all else a man of peace. Violence seemed to him a betrayal of the Gospel, whether it were committed by troops in India or by miners in the Welsh valleys. Force was a denial of all that socialism stood for. He believed that the ultimate object of the socialist movement was to avert war, and that the best way of achieving permanent peace abroad was the abolition of private capitalism at home. In fact, Britain had not been involved in a major war in Europe since 1815, and Hardie inherited a good deal of the optimism of his generation that a permanent peace would endure.

He was therefore deeply concerned with the growth of two mighty armed camps in Europe before 1914. The Triple Alliance of Germany, Austria–Hungary, and Italy confronted the Triple Entente of Britain, France, and Russia. People's minds were being poisoned, he thought, by war 'scares' in the Press, such as that whipped up by Harmsworth's *Daily Mail* on behalf of 'Dreadnought' battleships. He attacked Haldane at the War Office and Churchill at the Admiralty for committing the country to a reckless arms race. However, if the war fever was growing

in strength, so too was the peace movement. Radicals were vocal
in demanding a system of international law, and an end of secret
diplomacy which was regarded as a cause of war. The English
economist, Norman Angell, argued powerfully in *The Great
Illusion* that war was completely pointless, since it was as economically ruinous to the victors as to the vanquished. Hardie
himself was an ardent apostle of the peace movement; as we have
seen (Chapter 6), he conducted a crusade in the Socialist International on behalf of a strike against war. As militarism was the
ugly offspring of capitalism, so the consequence of socialism
would be a world at peace.

Hardie strongly attacked the foreign policy of Sir Edward
Grey: he claimed that it made war almost inevitable. In particular, he denounced the alliance with Tsarist Russia, to socialists
the most hateful of all tyrannies. After all, in 1906 thousands of
radicals and socialists there had been imprisoned or murdered
for taking part in political demonstrations during the 'Duma' (or
Parliament). Thousands of Russian Jews had been wiped out in
atrocious 'pogroms'. Russia was in no sense, Hardie considered, a
suitable ally for Britain. In June 1908 he protested violently in
the Commons against King Edward VII's visit to the Tsar; for
this, Hardie was rebuked by the Speaker. The King was most
indignant at this attack, and struck Hardie's name from the list
of those eligible for invitation to Buckingham Palace garden
parties. Hardie coolly replied that if he was fit to represent the
workers of Merthyr at Westminster, then he was a fit guest at
the Palace. The Labour Party staged a boycott of royal events,
the King gave way, and Hardie's name was restored.

Although international tension built up relentlessly, few really
thought war would come. Crises in 1905, 1908, and 1911 had somehow been overcome; somehow it was thought Europe would
totter back from the brink once more. But the sequence of events
that followed the assassination of the Archduke Franz Ferdinand
of Austria at Sarajevo (in Bosnia, part of modern Yugoslavia) on
28 June 1914, sucked all the great powers of Europe into a mael-
strom of conflict. By the beginning of August, it was obvious that
war was terrifyingly near at hand.

In the *Labour Leader*, Hardie urged the workers of Britain to strike against the war. In a great anti-war meeting, held in pouring rain at Trafalgar Square on 2 August 1914, he, Henderson, Lansbury, and others demanded that Britain should on no account intervene. But the next day, Grey told the Commons of the German invasion of Belgium and of the British ultimatum. If Germany did not withdraw, there would be war. Hardie courageously protested, as did Ramsay MacDonald, but to no avail. More and more Labour men followed the 'patriotic' line. Lloyd George and other radicals in Cabinet who had hesitated, chose to stay in the Government. In Europe, the façade of international socialist solidarity crumbled. In France, the mighty Jaurès had been assassinated and his followers rushed to join the 'Sacred Union' in defence of their fatherland. In Germany, almost all the Social Democrats in Parliament voted for war credits. In Britain, only a few I.L.P. men, headed by Hardie, MacDonald, and Snowden, stood out against the passions of the time. Morley and Burns were the only Cabinet ministers to resign; Burns's action, indeed, reconciled him to Hardie after many years of estrangement. And so Britain lurched into war on 4 August 1914. Asquith said it would be all over by Christmas. In fact, it was to drag on for over four terrible years, to cost over twelve million in killed and wounded (nearly 750,000 killed from Britain alone), and to wreak devastation and suffering on a scale unparalleled in the history of the world.

The outbreak of the war crushed Hardie in body and spirit. He had been in physical decline for many years; the war now shattered his will to live. Two days after war was declared, he held an anti-war demonstration in Aberdare, in his own constituency. It was broken up by an angry mob, and Hardie had to flee for his life. Some of those miners who had most recently urged violence against the coal-owners were now most ardent for war. Violence begat violence. Hardie remarked to a Merthyr friend that he now understood as well as any man the sufferings of Christ at Gethsemane.

Hardie felt too broken to carry on the kind of crusade he had led against the war in South Africa. His meetings at Merthyr were met by charges that he was a traitor, a friend of the 'Huns' and of every country save his own. He was denounced when he exposed, as the fantastic inventions they were, stories of German atrocities—tales of the mutilation of little children, the melting down of prisoners' bodies to make margarine, and the use of dead nuns as clappers inside bells. He was attacked in the House for having allegedly discouraged recruiting. Once again, the rights of free speech were being whittled away; liberty was the first casualty of war. By the end of 1914, Hardie was critically ill; Lord Morley was shocked by his appearance when they met briefly in the Commons lobby. His last speech on 25 February 1915 condemned the relaxing of educational by-laws to force children to work in agriculture; to the last he was a champion of the children. His last question in the House (27 April) demanded a rise in old age pensions. He spoke with difficulty and was barely audible. He also intervened briefly at the Norwich I.L.P. conference in April, denouncing the war as 'a disgrace to civilization'. In the *Labour Leader* and in the *Merthyr Pioneer,* he continued his courageous opposition to militarism. Soon afterwards, he fell even more seriously ill, and was taken away to his beloved Cumnock home in Scotland. There he died of pneumonia on 26 September 1915, at the age of fifty-nine.

At the end, Hardie regarded his life's work as utterly wasted. He was succeeded in the representation of Merthyr by a violent trade unionist, C. B. Stanton, who vented abuse on 'the filthy murderous Huns' and the 'brutal butchers of Berlin'. The war dragged on its savage course for a further three years. At the next general election in November 1918, Lloyd George won a huge majority in a 'jingo' campaign in which ministers advocated the hanging of the Kaiser and 'squeezing Germany till the pips squeaked'. What had happened to Hardie's crusade for international brotherhood in this torrent of nationalist hatred? *The Times* in its obituary summed him up as 'one of those doomed to spend their lives in expressing the views of a minority'. He had always been an extremist, it declared. 'No speaker has had more meetings broken up in more continents than he.' The 'coupon' general election of 1918 seemed to provide the last futile comment on his career.

In fact, the war hysteria soon passed away. Britain was not essentially a warlike country in normal times. By 1966, almost all the causes for which Hardie laboured had been won—with the significant exception that peace seemed as far away as ever, and threatened by weapons more hideous than any Hardie could have imagined. Abroad, in 1947 India gained self-government, along with Pakistan, Burma, and Ceylon. At home, women have had the vote since 1918. The welfare state is now beyond party controversy, with old age pensions, a national health service, social insurance, a miners' eight-hour day, and other social reforms firmly on the statute book. The public ownership of major industries, and policies to try to protect full employment seem almost equally secure. The Labour Party has risen from being a small minority in 1915 to become one of the two major parties, which has now held office on four occasions (1924, 1929–31, 1945–51, and since 1964). It no longer seems shocking or revolutionary, but is as respectable and parliamentary as any other party. When in the autumn of 1965, Dr. Horace King was elected as the first Labour Speaker, the veteran Scottish member, Emanuel Shinwell, reflected that Keir Hardie (himself a scourge of Speakers) would have been proud to see that day. How much the Labour Party has lost in this progress towards respectable acceptance is open to debate.

Hardie would have liked to think that these triumphs were the result of growing public enlightenment and moral concern. In part, this may have been so. Yet the irony was that in large measure the progress gained was helped on by the very forces that Hardie most detested, namely the effects of two world wars. The First World War brought not only unparalleled devastation but also immense gains for the working class. Trade unions grew much more powerful; wages went up, working hours went down; Labour replaced the Liberals as spokesmen for the British left. The Second World War brought with it a new passion for social equality, with notable documents like the Beveridge Report of 1942 with its comprehensive scheme for social security. The welfare state and full employment owe as much to the horrors of war as to the enlightenment of peace. One wonders what Hardie would have made of it all.

His contribution to the British labour movement was two-fold above all. First, he was a great party tactician, whose leadership was vital in building up an independent party in the years before 1906. He was the supreme architect of the coalition between the socialist societies and the trade unions. Although the main founder of the I.L.P., he also saw, perhaps more clearly than anyone else at the time, that any mass working-class movement in Britain must be constructed on the base of the older Liberalism, with which the unions were closely identified. After 1906, he was a major force in keeping the new Party on constitutional lines, steering a middle course between Hyndman and the Webbs. He was a shrewd and realistic man, who saw the need for a struggling party to work with Liberal allies, even though others accused him of 'class betrayal'. His own election for Merthyr Tydfil owed much to the votes of active chapel-going Liberals. This down-to-earth realism, attempting to adapt socialist principles to a native British setting, helped to make the Labour Party the leading democratic socialist party in the world after 1918.

Secondly, Hardie was the prophet and evangelist, who could sway mass audiences in a manner given to few of his contemporaries. He had a unique command over the working-class mind; he was among the first to make the football crowds politically articulate. The Labour Party, he wrote in his *Confession of Faith*, is 'an uprising of the working class, overseered and guided by men of that class, painfully and slowly working out its own emancipation'. He lent the labour movement in Britain, and in many other countries, a moral fervour and a self-confidence that gave it impetus in later years. As a pamphleteer and even more as a public speaker, Hardie could express the deep, emotional force behind working-class culture, shining through the gloom of industrial society. In the Commons he was less at home, though some of his speeches, for instance on India and on unemployment, focussed attention on vital issues neglected at the time. Basically, he was not a parliamentarian at all, but, in Bruce Glasier's phrase, 'an agitator, an apostle, a champion, a pioneer'. It was left to Ramsay MacDonald after 1918 to turn Labour from an incoherent 'movement' into a real political force.

As a man, Hardie was more complex than at first appeared. One associate, S. G. Hobson, found him moody: 'the cheery word too frequently gave way to the surly growl'. Hardie wrote of himself, 'I am of the unfortunate class who never knew what it was to be a child in spirit. Even the memories of boyhood and young manhood are gloomy.' Yet he was far more than a mere dismal puritan. He had a real sense of humour, especially as he mellowed with age; the comedy as well as the tragedy of life could move him. He was in his way deeply religious, though Philip Snowden noted that he was also superstitious; he kept lucky charms and believed he had lived before in some former incarnation. He could be deeply sentimental, moved to tears by cruelty to children or to animals, yet hard, even ruthless, in crushing political opponents. His speeches and writings were littered with terms such as 'parasites' or 'hirelings of the privileged class'. Perhaps he felt most at home among his fellow Scots. A man like Bruce Glasier understood him in all his moods, in his moments of depression as well as his periods of sunny optimism. To the general public, the impression was above all of an honourable, courageous man, quite incorruptible. Frank Hodges, the miners' leader, noted Hardie's calm in the face of a yelling, violent mob of Oxford students: 'What infinite patience! What abysmal pity!' Countless others could have echoed those words.

When Hardie died, Bernard Shaw observed that while he lay mouldering in his grave, like John Brown's body his soul would go marching on. Few have more profoundly influenced the course of the British working-class movement, political and industrial, than has Keir Hardie. His simple creed of human fellowship and Christian brotherhood, stemming from the older Liberalism, has done far more to build up the British Labour Party than any more complicated philosophy—certainly far more than Marxism whose influence in Britain has been comparatively slight. Hardie was not a profound political or economic thinker. Few of his numerous tracts on socialism have added much to the history of socialist thought. His vision of 'merrie England' appealed to the heart rather than to the head: 'England without a sweated, miserable drudge, without a pauper; her old people, honoured and beloved; her young people, industrious, temperate and healthy; each Englishman and Englishwoman . . . not working for self but for the general good.' He was much less clear on how to bring this happy state of affairs about. It is not through his ideas but rather through the force of his personality, and through the institutions he created, that his work has lived on to inspire those who came after him. As class barriers slowly dissolve in Britain in the later twentieth century, Hardie will be remembered as a man of the people who never forgot his origins, a crusader for the downtrodden and the outcast throughout the world. Perhaps the man of integrity ultimately achieves more in politics than does the man of intellect. If this be so, then the life of Keir Hardie, with all its disappointments and all its unhappiness, has been a truly decisive force in the shaping of modern Britain and the world we know today.

PRINCIPAL DATES

1856 Born in Legbrannock, Lanarkshire, 15 August.
1866 Entered the mine as a trapper.
1879 Appointed agent of Hamilton miners.
1880 'Tattie strike' in Lanarkshire.
1882 Joins staff of *Cumnock News*.
1886 Appointed organizing secretary of Ayrshire miners, and secretary of Scottish Miners' Federation.
1887 Founds *The Miner*.
     Attends Swansea T.U.C.
1888 Mid-Lanark by-election (27 April); Scottish Labour Party formed.
1892 Elected M.P. for West Ham (South).
1893 I.L.P. formed at Bradford (13–14 January).
1894 *Labour Leader* becomes a weekly (31 March).
1895 Defeated at West Ham; first visit to United States.
1898 Visits South Wales during six-months' coal stoppage.
1900 Formation of L.R.C. (27 February). Defeated at Preston, but returned as M.P. for Merthyr Tydfil.
1903 Gives up editorship of *Labour Leader*.
1906 Re-elected for Merthyr Tydfil. Elected first chairman of Parliamentary Labour Party.
1907 Journey round the world—Canada, India, Australia, S. Africa.
1909 Resigns from I.L.P. executive.
1910 International Socialist Congress at Copenhagen. Riots at Tonypandy (7–8 November).
1912 Final visit to the United States.
1914 Presides at I.L.P. coming-of-age conference at Bradford. Leads demonstrations against First World War.
1915 Dies in Cumnock, 26 September.

FOR FURTHER READING

THE best and most recent of the many lives of Keir Hardie is Emrys Hughes, *Keir Hardie* (1956). (Mr. Hughes, Labour M.P. for South Ayrshire, married Nan, Hardie's daughter). This book has many extracts from Hardie's speeches and writings and a deep personal affection for its subject. The same author's *Pictorial Biography of Keir Hardie* (1950) contains many excellent photographs. Of the older biographies, William Stewart, *J. Keir Hardie* (1921), with an introduction by Ramsay MacDonald, is rambling and shapeless, but is a mine of valuable information, much of it based on the author's personal acquaintance. David Lowe, *From Pit to Parliament: the story of the early life of Keir Hardie* (1923) has some useful details on Hardie's career up to 1900, but is of less value than the same writer's *Memorials of Scottish Labour* (1919). Of the shorter accounts of Hardie's career, J. Bruce Glasier, *Keir Hardie: the Man and his Message* (1919) is a moving tribute from a close personal friend. Francis Johnson, *Keir Hardie's Socialism* (1922) and Hamilton Fyfe, *Keir Hardie* (1935) both cover well-trodden ground in a very readable way. James Maxton, *Keir Hardie: Prophet and Pioneer* (1939) and G. D. H. Cole, *Keir Hardie* (1941) are two useful sketches. John Cockburn, *The Hungry Heart: a romantic biography of Keir Hardie* (1956) makes no claim to be a work of history, but conveys vividly the atmosphere of Hardie's childhood. There is a helpful anthology in *Keir Hardie's Speeches and Writings, 1888–1915* (edited by Emrys Hughes, 1928); Hardie is also represented in *A Socialist Anthology* (edited by Norman Longmate, 1951) and *The Challenge of Socialism* (edited by Henry Pelling, 1954). The most thorough general introduction is Henry Pelling, *The Origins of the Labour Party* (1954). Two very useful recent articles are James G. Kellas, 'The Mid-Lanark By-Election (1888) and the Scottish Labour Party (1888–1894)', *Parliamentary Affairs*, Summer, 1965; and Kenneth O. Fox, 'Labour and Merthyr's Khaki Election of 1900', *Welsh History Review*, vol. 2, no. 4 (1965).

INDEX